James Wallace Anderson

Lectures on medical Nursing

Delivered in the Royal Infirmary, Glasgow

James Wallace Anderson

Lectures on medical Nursing
Delivered in the Royal Infirmary, Glasgow

ISBN/EAN: 9783337163112

Printed in Europe, USA, Canada, Australia, Japan

Cover: Foto ©ninafisch / pixelio.de

More available books at **www.hansebooks.com**

MEDICAL NURSING.

Published by
JAMES MACLEHOSE AND SONS, GLASGOW,
𝔓ublishers to the 𝔘niversity.

LONDON: MACMILLAN AND CO.

London,	*Hamilton, Adams & Co.*
Cambridge,	*Macmillan & Bowes.*
Edinburgh,	*Douglas & Foulis.*
Dublin,	*Fannin & Co.*
New York,	*Macmillan & Co.*

MDCCCLXXXIII.

LECTURES

ON

MEDICAL NURSING

DELIVERED IN THE ROYAL INFIRMARY, GLASGOW

BY

J. WALLACE ANDERSON, M.D.

LECTURER ON MEDICINE, ROYAL INFIRMARY MEDICAL SCHOOL, AND
PHYSICIAN TO THE ROYAL INFIRMARY DISPENSARY, GLASGOW

GLASGOW:
JAMES MACLEHOSE & SONS, ST. VINCENT STREET,
Publishers to the University.
1883.

All rights reserved.

To

WILLIAM M'EWEN, ESQ.,
CHAIRMAN OF HOUSE COMMITTEE, ROYAL INFIRMARY,

THESE LECTURES ARE

DEDICATED,

IN APPRECIATION OF HIS INTEREST IN THE WORK OF
WHICH THEY HAVE FORMED A PART,

AND IN ACKNOWLEDGMENT OF WISE COUNSEL
KINDLY GIVEN.

PREFACE.

FIVE years ago the Managers of the Glasgow Royal Infirmary resolved that a course of Systematic Lectures on Nursing should be added to the practical training, that, for many years previously, the nurse probationers of the hospital had in turn undergone. It was arranged that I should undertake the medical section of the work; and since then I have given, once a year or oftener, a course of lectures on Medical Nursing. Now that other duties prevent me continuing these lectures, I have thought that in this form they may continue to be of some service, and to a greater number. They are here presented exactly as they were delivered during the present autumn, with the exception of the last, which formed the concluding lecture of a previous course.

The questions appended to each lecture are not exhaustive, and are intended chiefly for those who are unaccustomed to have their knowledge tested by any kind of examination, or who may be, for a time, studying the theory of the subject unaided. They will recall to a few who read them hard and earnest work: they remind me of valuable and valued aid unsparingly given. I was never present at any of the tutorial meetings; I only know that on repeated evenings between each lecture, notes were compared and corrected, and the more difficult points cleared up, mainly by means of questions such as these. Mrs. Strong, our matron, and some of her past and present assistants, know much more about this than I do.

With regard to the manner in which the work has been done, I may be allowed to anticipate this objection—that too much has been taught. I shall only say that I have had that danger always before my mind, and that I think I have avoided it. There is a very old French proverb which says, *Assez n'y a, si trop n'y a;* and there is nothing to which it is more applicable than to the teaching of the care of the sick.

GLASGOW, *October*, 1882.

CONTENTS.

LECTURE I.

HISTORY OF MODERN NURSING—RECENT VIEWS OF DISEASE—THE CONSTANT AND SKILLED CARE OF THE SICK—A NURSE'S DUTY TO THE DOCTOR AND TO THE PATIENT—NECESSITY OF OBSERVATION—WHAT TO OBSERVE, ... 1

LECTURE II.

TEMPERATURE—PULSE—ITS RELATION TO STIMULANTS—RESPIRATION, ... 21

LECTURE III.

COUGH—EXPECTORATION—HÆMOPTYSIS—HÆMATEMESIS—VENTILATION—FOOD OR DIET, . . 39

LECTURE IV.

THE DIGESTION OF FOOD—PRACTICAL LESSONS TO BE DRAWN—DIGESTIBILITY OF DIFFERENT FORMS OF DIET—THE COOKING OF FOOD—THE ADMINISTRATION OF FOOD, ... 59

LECTURE V.

THE CARE OF SPECIAL DISEASES, MAINLY AS REGARDS DIET: DIARRHŒA—SCURVY—RICKETS—SCROFULA—RHEUMATISM—ANEURISM—DIABETES: GENERAL REFERENCE TO DISEASES OF THE KIDNEY, ... 79

LECTURE VI.

THE EXAMINATION OF THE URINE—CHARACTER OF THE MOTIONS FROM THE BOWELS—THE NERVOUS SYSTEM AND ITS DISEASES—APOPLEXY—EPILEPSY—FAINTING—PARALYSIS, . . . 100

LECTURE VII.

THE INFECTIOUS FEVERS—TYPHUS FEVER—ENTERIC FEVER—SCARLET FEVER—MEASLES—HOOPING COUGH—DIPHTHERIA, . . . 119

LECTURE VIII.

THE PREVENTION OF BEDSORES: EXTERNAL APPLICATIONS—FOMENTATIONS—POULTICES—A FLY BLISTER—DRY HEAT—COLD LOTION—THE APPLICATION OF ICE—THE COLD COMPRESS, . . 140

LECTURE IX.

BATHS—THE COLD PACK—COLD AFFUSION—LEECHES—ENEMATA—HYPODERMIC INJECTIONS—THE ADMINISTRATION OF INTERNAL REMEDIES, . 160

LECTURE X.

CONCLUDING REMARKS—NATURAL QUALIFICATIONS OF A NURSE—THE CULTIVATION OF CERTAIN HABITS—HABITS TO BE AVOIDED—THE RELATION BETWEEN DOCTOR, NURSE, AND PATIENT, . 179

APPENDIX—

INVALID COOKERY, ...	199
PEPTONISED FOODS, ...	208
POISONS AND ANTIDOTES, ...	211
WEIGHTS AND FLUID MEASURES, . . .	214
GLOSSARY OF MEDICAL TERMS, . . .	215

NURSING.

LECTURE I.

HISTORY OF MODERN NURSING—RECENT VIEWS OF DISEASE—THE CONSTANT AND SKILLED CARE OF THE SICK—A NURSE'S DUTY TO THE DOCTOR AND TO THE PATIENT—NECESSITY OF OBSERVATION—WHAT TO OBSERVE.

YOU have all formed some idea of what your duties will be as nurses of the sick. You are here to-day because others have told you about the work, and their report has been a good one. You have therefore chosen it for your own calling and now you are looking earnestly ahead. Shall I be fit for it? Shall I like it? Shall I succeed in it? These are the questions you are asking yourselves. They are questions that cannot be answered yet; but of this you may be sure, that all who have the oversight of you, will help you to fit yourselves for the work, and wish to help you to like it, and help you to succeed in it. The importance of good nursing is being more and more fully recognised every day. People are talking about it. We sometimes hear of the workers not being all that could be wished, but the work is none the less there to be done—there for you to do all the better.

Nursing has not been always viewed in this way. Not so long a time ago but that some of us here may remember it, any woman of somewhat advanced years and "who had seen a deal of trouble herself," was considered on these grounds qualified to undertake the duties of a sick nurse. But those days are past, and there is nothing to be gained by recalling the stories we have heard about them. Let us look rather into the history of nursing, that we may trace the steps by which it has attained to its present honourable and important position.

Before attempting to determine what may

be considered the beginning of modern nursing, let me direct your attention to two circumstances which bear directly on its origin. In all ages we find that the condition of the wounded in battle has called forth the sympathies and action of at least a few, who have ministered as best they could to the wants of the sufferers. It never led, however, to any united action to render the care and treatment more effective. Then there is that growing spirit of humanity which characterised the close of the last and the beginning of the present century. You know what work was done by such philanthropists as Howard and Wilberforce and Mrs. Fry. The slave was set free, the vicious and degraded were cared for and rescued, where that was possible, from the evil into which they had fallen. But the sick and wounded had as yet no such champions of their cause. Those who had fought our battles and had fallen, were passed by. But out of war on the one hand, and that spirit of benevolence, to which we have referred, on the other, modern nursing clearly arose. The work done by a few German ladies amongst the wounded in the disastrous battles of Prussia with the first Napoleon led, years afterwards, to the foundation of the systematic nursing of the sick in Germany. We find, too, that a visit to the field of Waterloo, in 1816, forced upon the poet Southey the conviction that some attention should be devoted to hospitals, *as well as to poorhouses*, and in 1829 he was in correspondence with Mrs. Fry and others, not about prisons now alone, but regarding the internal management of hospitals. But little came of that and other similar projects, and we must go out of our own country to find the real beginning of the systematic training of nurses.

It dates from 1836 when Theodore Fliedner, the pastor of a small Protestant Congregation at Kaiserswerth on the Rhine, established in that little German village what he called the Deaconess Institution. There under the superintendence of himself and his wife, a training school for female nurses was begun. It was carried on from the first in a markedly devotional spirit and was based on the principle of the Deaconess Institutions of the Early

Church.* Fliedner's Institution was therefore quite a religious community, but with no vows, as the founder always said; the only bond of union being the Word of God. It still flourishes along with many others on the Continent which have followed in its path, and has been the training school of many a leader of the work in our own country. Pastor Fliedner died in 1864. I think there can be no doubt he is entitled to be considered the founder of modern nursing.

War again gave the next, and, in the case of our own country, the first great impulse to the proper care of the sick. Everyone has read about, or knows something of the sufferings of our soldiers in the Crimea. It was not that more than 3000 men died from wounds received in action—this is looked upon as the inevitable result of war—but that

* There is good reason to believe that in the Apostolic Church such a community existed, and that Dorcas, Priscilla, Phœbe, and many others were members of such a society. Phœbe is expressly called a "deaconess" (*diakonos*, in Greek)—a *minister* or *servant* of the church (Rom. xvi, 1). It was probably a part of their duty to visit and attend the sick.

six times that number should have died of other diseases, largely preventible, which was felt to be a national disgrace. And when a lady was found who was able to meet and successfully grapple with the emergency, everyone looked to her, and thought of what she had done, with quite a personal interest. On the 21st October, 1854, Miss Nightingale left England for the Crimea, with a staff of thirty-seven nurses, and within two years she was back again, having won the gratitude and admiration of the whole army. Her name was a household word in every soldier's home, and soon also in every home in the land. So it was that, in our own country, universal attention came to be directed to the proper care of the sick.

In Willis's Rooms, London, on the 29th November, 1855, a great meeting was held to arrange about a form of testimonial to Miss Nightingale which should be truly national in its character. It resulted before long in a large sum of money being collected, which was called "The Nightingale Fund." This Miss Nightingale refused to accept for herself, but suggested that it should be placed in the hands of Trustees for an object she had greatly at heart, and which she would herself supervise—the training of nurses. This being done, arrangements were at last made between the Nightingale Fund Committee and the Treasurer and Governors of St. Thomas's Hospital, and on the 9th June, 1860, Miss Nightingale's Training School was opened in that hospital with eight probationers.

This leads me to say a word or two of one whose name, well known as it is, is not so widely known in the north here as it deserves to be—I mean Mrs. Wardroper, the matron of St. Thomas's Hospital. Before the Crimean war had made sick-nursing a subject of common remark, Mrs. Wardroper's attention had been directed to the general character and position of the hospital nurse, as not at all befitting the nature and requirements of such an important calling. That lady recognised that a nurse must be trained; that the care of the sick was a higher duty, was a more important and more responsible work than could be done by those who were expected to perform, in addition, many menial duties. After many endeavours to improve generally the nurse's position in hospital, and have her work confined exclusively to attendance on the patients, Mrs. Wardroper was allowed to put her ideas into practice, and what is known as "The New System" of nursing was introduced into St. Thomas's Hospital in 1858. It very soon proved a success. Miss Nightingale recognised this when in 1860 she selected St. Thomas's as her Training School.

Meanwhile others had begun to work on the same lines, and gradually "The New System" extended itself from the metropolis over the whole country.

But while good men and women were taking pity on the sick, and carrying out plans for their better nursing, the medical profession was taking a new view of disease itself, which tended in the same direction. It was being understood that disease was not a mighty but indefinite something, that must be charmed away or driven from the system by some powerful medicine; but rather and simply a departure from health, the return to which must be invited by gentle persuasion and aided by incessant care. This, at least, is very much the position taken up now, one which obviously calls for special qualifications and special training, *besides*, though not *over and above*, a doctor's skill.

You are aware that the duties upon which you have entered will bring you continually face to face with disease. It is in the conflict with it that you have determined to take part. We all know too well what is understood by the term disease, and I am not going to attempt to tell you what it actually is, further than what I have already said, that it is a greater or less departure from that condition which we call health. But I think it will help you to understand your duty in the matter, if you keep before your mind the idea of a conflict. There are on the one side our vital powers which tend to health, on the other countless foes continually about us, which tend to propagate disease. It is on the side of health you fight, or we might say rather, in support of a great force or power within us which always inclines to health.

This power has received many names, but none better than one given to it long ago —*the healing power of Nature*. I am not going to discuss with you what this power is. I could not do so simply, and therefore only commend it to you as a principle which it is well to recognise.

You might then accept this from me as a maxim, that given a condition of disease, Nature always inclines to return to that state which we call health. I say inclines, for sometimes, too often, she cannot actually return. But that Nature ever endeavours to effect this return is a safe position to take, and a sound basis for all our care of the sick. For we shall not fail in our duty if we understand that in every possible way we must strengthen Nature's hand, and remove all obstacles in her path. So, on the other hand, must we watch for every possible form of attack on the part of disease, and meet, so far as we can, every inroad actually made. And it is just because the attacks and the inroads may be made at any time that the watch must be incessant, and for this reason we need your care. But the attacks, too, are of every kind and often obscurely made. We need, therefore, not only incessant care, but skilled care—we need not only nurses, but trained nurses.

Such is the general view of your work that I can with most confidence commend to you. Let us now consider your duties more specially. Here we are confronted with a very wide question, and the first division I would make of it is into duties coming directly under the doctor's supervision, what we might call professional duties, and those with which he is only indirectly, often very indirectly, concerned. This latter division includes all excluded by the former; includes all that I think should be excluded by the medical lecturer, and left to those who are alone competent to advise you upon them—the matron and her assistants.

Confining our attention, then, to those which may be called professional duties, we divide them into—I. Your duty to the doctor; and II. Your duty to the patient.

I. Your duty to the doctor. We may put it shortly thus, *To report on the past and take his instructions for the future;* or, more at length, to be able intelligently to report on the patient's condition since the doctor's last visit, and understand and carry out his instructions till he returns.

II. Your duty to the patient. *To watch and tend him.* That is a definition short enough and comprehensive enough, if by *watching* we are to understand protecting our patient as an object that he comes to no harm, and by *tending*, ministering to his wants as a living being. The duty is generally and very well put somewhat in this way—to obtain the most favourable conditions possible for the patient, as regards, for example, food, rest, air, warmth, cleanliness, &c.*

Such may be taken as a general expression of your professional duties, and a little reflection will convince you that it involves a countless number of individual duties, none of which can be overlooked. No duty is little or trifling with such interests at stake as we have to deal with. To help you to recognise them, and their importance when you do see

* Miss Nightingale and others.

them, is the object of these lectures. The *seeing* of them is the essential thing, and that is what each of you must do for herself. You must use your *own* eyes; and you must be careful that you *do* use them. That is the point we come to now, but I shall put it in other words—*cultivate the habit of observation.*

Observation is what we all begin with: it is the first step to the knowledge of anything. But I can imagine no kind of work in which observation is of more special importance than in yours; with you it must be first in importance, as it is first in order with all. You must cultivate it then, and cultivate it into a habit. It is wonderful to what an extent observation can be cultivated. Houdin, the well-known conjurer, tells us he did so for the purposes of his art. He began by trying how many volumes he could note the names of in passing a bookseller's window at the ordinary pace. Very soon he could observe and remember the name of every one placed side by side in a line in the window, by simply catching the title of each as he ran his eyes along the row; and he gradually developed this power to a much greater degree.

Now I can assure you that you are all capable of cultivating this power. You do not require to go to a shop window to do so, or be in any hurry about it. You have only in the ward or by the bedside to note quietly whatever you think is noteworthy, and the power will grow to a degree that will astonish yourselves. In the surgical wards you have the greater opportunity of direct observation of disease, and you generally therefore begin your training there. You are expected to use your eyes and take a mental note of what you see, that you may train yourselves to that degree of observation that will enable you to give a good report of a case when that is required of you. On the medical side you will find this as a rule a more difficult thing to do. For as your observation is less direct so must it be the more comprehensive. For example, you will not have to note for the doctor's information when the blush of redness was first observed in the vicinity of the wound, but such a thing as, say, some slight peculiarity of expression, or an ill defined change in the character of the breathing.

The question then—What am I to observe?—is a wide one, and to answer it in some way is the object we have in view. I shall keep that question before my mind throughout all the lectures, and make them the answer to it, so far as the subject will admit of being treated in that way. But before taking up the matter in detail, I should like to present it to you in a somewhat tabular form, merely sketching in outline a few points as they occur to me, which will help to guide you in your study of the whole subject.

First, I would remark that it is not necessary you should note any appearance or condition concerning the patient which is more or less constant, but rather such *changes* as may occur in his condition during the doctor's absence. You do not require to note, for example, that the patient is of a scrofulous constitution; but you are expected to observe that he perspires very much at night, should such be the case. Indeed, we might say that his general condition is only noteworthy on your part that you may appreciate any *change* in it. And so for that reason it *is* necessary that you should take note of the general appearance of the patient and form an opinion regarding his manner, temper &c. Is he cheerful or dull, listless or anxious, quiet or restless? Endeavour to form an opinion on such general points as these, and note carefully any alteration in them; for it may indicate a distinct turn or *crisis* in the disease, or that a new stage has been reached; or further, that a serious outbreak is approaching in some form of mental disorder.

Another general conclusion to be arrived at is the patient's estimate or expression of pain or discomfort. I am not speaking of pain itself, (we shall consider that immediately under the special points); but does he *bear* pain well, or is he simply a grumbler. We may have complaint without pain—that we all know; but we may also have real pain endured without complaint of any kind. This latter feature is so comparatively uncommon that it is apt to be altogether overlooked.

We have now to consider some special conditions which come under observation, or rather, as I have said, alterations in the patient's condition which must be noted.

1. The amount and depth of the colour of the face. These may indicate not only the degree of feverishness, but a particular fever. Any change of colour or appearance of the face, apart from what is understood as a flush, should be noted; for example, the yellow tinge in the white-of-the-eye, which is one of the earliest symptoms of jaundice; changes in expression from paralysis of certain muscles of the face, &c. 2. The state of the skin, particularly as regards perspiration. This latter is sometimes the accompaniment of a decided change for the better, as at the turn or crisis of a fever; sometimes it is an aggravation of the disease and indicates increasing weakness. It is often confined to the head, especially in children. 3. The character of the breathing, and of the cough and expectoration, if any. This is of great importance in all chest affections, and will be referred to in detail in the lecture after next. In this connection is to be noted

also any change in, or peculiarity of posture in bed. You would remark, for example, the fact of a patient finding that he can now lie most easily on what was previously the painful side, and on which he could not possibly lie before. 4. Pain. Its character, time of occurrence, and its situation, must always be carefully noted. If not continuous, note if it returns invariably about the same hour of the day or night. The character of pain is endless in variety, and a great number of terms are used to express different kinds, such as dull, aching, burning, throbbing, darting, &c. In mentioning these, I have a fitting opportunity of giving you an important caution and at the same time a sound general rule. Never suggest to a patient a description of a symptom or symptoms to which your attention is drawn. You may find it necessary to help him to explain himself; but as a rule his own very words, however grotesque they may appear to you, are of the highest value to you in reporting the matter afterwards to the doctor. 5. All points connected with the patient's appetite for food and with what he does take, are of great importance, and will be considered by and bye. 6. The state of the excretions. In many diseases the examination of the stools and of the urine is of great importance, and in any case peculiarities in them should be carefully noted. 7. The amount and character of the sleep. Whether sleeplessness and unrest; or an undue amount of sleep and general drowsiness.

These may be taken as an example of the kind of things you have to observe, but they and many others will be considered more at length afterwards.

I shall conclude with a caution that applies to all I have been saying about observation. Remember that as nurses you have only facts to observe, and not opinions to form. That is why I said that for you, observation was first in importance as well as first in order. Of course as individuals you must form opinions, but as nurses you are not to act upon them. It is the doctor's opinion you follow. He has the causes, nature, symptoms, and treatment of disease to study; you have only the symptoms to observe, and the treatment faithfully to carry out.

QUESTIONS ON LECTURE I.

1. Mention the principal steps which have led to the present position of sick nursing.

2. What position should a nurse take with reference to disease?

3. What is understood by the "healing power of nature"?

4. Define a nurse's duty to the doctor and to the patient.

5. Why should a nurse cultivate the habit of exact observation?

6. Mention what was said about the observation of the patient's general condition.

7. Give some special points that should be noted.

LECTURE II.

Temperature—Pulse—Its Relation to Stimulants—Respiration.

Keeping observation before us as our theme, I begin to-day with the observation of:— The Temperature of the body. The temperature or heat of the body has of late years attracted much attention as being a very valuable means of diagnosis.* It is so, because in health the temperature is so constant. Whether we be in the sunny South or amidst perpetual snows, if we are in health, our temperature is practically the same. We say we feel the heat, or our hands are benumbed with cold; but the temperature of our blood or of the internal parts of our body is not mate-

---

* Diagnosis, the knowledge or recognition of disease, or of a disease.

rially affected by such diverse external conditions. On the other hand, one of the first indications of disease is a rise of temperature, possibly such a rise as only the thermometer can detect, the patient himself perhaps feeling nothing wrong, or at most a sense of chilliness in place of the feverishness which is actually developing. But another reason why it is so valuable a means of diagnosis is because we have an exact method of ascertaining it, and this duty being now almost invariably left to the trained nurse, it is well that we should consider it thus early.

The temperature of the body, or of anything, is ascertained or taken, as we say, by means of the thermometer. I do not require to describe it to you in detail, for you will find one in every ward. Suppose you take up one in your warm hand, you will notice that the mercury in the bulb at one end will begin to rise up into a fine tube, which you can see, extends to the other end of the instrument. This depends on the natural law which applies to all matter, that heat causes expansion. The wheelwright knows that heat expands the metal iron, when he makes the tire red hot, that on cooling it may contract again, and grasp the wheel more tightly. So does the metal mercury or quicksilver expand, and being, unlike most metals, a liquid, it expands to a greater degree by heat ; and for many other reasons it is the best substance for our purpose. Further, you will notice that the thermometer which we use has a very fine tube, so that a rise or fall, an expansion or contraction of the mercury, which we could not detect, for example, in the bulb at the end, is readily seen in the small column. We get in this way what we want ; an instrument that will plainly record for us a difference in the heat or temperature of the body, which we could never recognise by our touch, far less express in definite terms.

But while we can see that it rises and falls, we must have numbers to indicate the extent to which this occurs, if we wish to have definite terms, and we must have fixed numbers that will apply to all instruments, if we wish to have a uniform expression of a particular temperature. In our country the thermometer usually employed is known as Fahrenheit's, and it is so graduated or marked that the freezing point of water is thirty-two degrees (written 32°) and the boiling point 212°. By this scale the natural temperature of our body is about $98\frac{1}{2}°$, or, as it is usually expressed, 98 point 5 (written 98·5°). I believe the majority of you know that the figure after the point means so many tenths, 98·5° meaning 98 and $\frac{5}{10}$. Look now at a clinical thermometer, and you will see that each degree is divided into five parts or fifths (at least such is the usual subdivision), there being hardly space to mark off tenths. Look again at the degree marked 100. Suppose the mercury rises to the first of the smallest marks above the 100, it will indicate a temperature of 100 and $\frac{1}{5}$ or $\frac{2}{10}$, or, as we always read it, 100·2°. A little reflection and assistance from others will enable you all to understand this and to read any temperature in a similar way.

Before going further, notice here the arrowhead at one of the smaller marks above 98°.

This you will read as 98·4°—a number you must remember as being that of the average natural temperature of the body. The temperature of the human body in health varies somewhat in the twenty-four hours. It is rather higher in the afternoon than in the morning, and in disease this difference is, as a rule, increased. For this reason the temperature is usually taken morning and evening, to see if besides, say, a general rise, there is any peculiarity in the relation between the two. In hospital, before breakfast and before supper are generally the most convenient times for taking the temperature, but whatever be the time selected *it ought to be the same every day*. Should you be directed to do so more frequently, you will be told, or should ask, what hours you are to select.

We come now to the mode of taking the temperature. It will not do to lay the thermometer on any exposed surface of the body; for that is more or less cooled by contact with the external air. We must select a closed cavity, or what can be made one, in which the thermometer may lie. One or other of two parts of the body is usually selected for this purpose; the closed armpit (the *axilla*), or the end of the bowel (the *rectum*). The former is the more convenient; the latter perhaps gives the more reliable results. We shall first describe how to take the temperature in the axilla.

The patient being in bed and if possible lying on his back, the thermometer is taken by the stem and the bulb placed fairly into the hollow of the armpit. The arm is then brought close to the side, so that the bulb and, say, the lower half of the instrument are thereby held, and quite shut in, by the axilla; the forearm is now brought across the chest, and the whole side fixed in position by the patient grasping the elbow with the opposite hand.

The next question to be considered is, how long shall we keep the thermometer in the axilla? Shall it be five, ten, or fifteen minutes? That will depend entirely upon whether or not the axilla has been previously prepared, by being kept closed and covered from the air for some little time. If it has not, then obviously the axilla itself will take a certain time to rise to the temperature of a closed cavity of the body, and still a further time to raise the mercury to the proper height. Here then we are led to a little matter of detail which is really of great value to you in hospital, where you may have half-a-dozen or more temperatures to take in the morning. It is this. At least fifteen minutes before beginning, all the patients should be in bed, arms by the sides, and the bed-clothes carefully tucked in over the shoulders and round the neck. In this way the axilla will be, as we have said, prepared, and if this is done, five minutes, but on no account less, may be considered a sufficient time to keep the thermometer in. In other circumstances, ten minutes or a quarter of an hour may be required.

The only other precautions that need be added, are, to wipe the arm-pit dry should there be perspiration; to see that no clothes come between the instrument and the patient's body; and, in the case of children, or with very weak or delirious patients, to keep the thermometer and parts generally in the proper position. If taken in the rectum the bulb should be oiled, and passed about two inches into the bowel, and retained in position there for five minutes.

With the old form of thermometer, when the temperature was taken, it had to be read from the stem while the bulb was in position; because in taking out the instrument the very much colder atmosphere caused the mercury to run quickly down. All the clinical thermometers, however, now in use, are what is called *self-registering*. They are so made, that when the mercury runs down, a small portion, separated from the main column by a little bell of air, remains fixed; so that the temperature may not only be read on taking the instrument out, but at any time afterwards, if left undisturbed.

Having read off the temperature so registered, you note it down on a special card, or on a sheet of paper, with at least date and morning and evening temperature columns; the patient's name and the ward being written across the top. When you have done so, *you* must never forget to lower "*the index*," as we call the part of the mercury left at the top, before taking another; for should the next be a lower temperature, the index will of course remain at the original height, and you will have simply the record of the first temperature continued. Always, then, lower the index two or three degrees below the *normal* (or natural) temperature of the body. This you may do by taking the instrument in your hand, holding it by the upper half of the stem, bulb downwards, and shaking the index down by a succession of rapid swings of the arm downwards and backwards. This is also a handy way of breaking the thermometer, as you may readily swing it against something. In some respects, therefore, a better method is to grasp the thermometer with the right hand, in such a way as to have the bulb downwards and caught by the folds of the third and fourth fingers; and then bring this end of the fist smartly down on the palm of the left hand until the index is sufficiently lowered.

Such are the details which it is essential you should remember and understand, if you are to be trusted, as a thoroughly trained nurse, to take a temperature. The import of certain temperatures does not greatly concern you. I would only say that when a temperature reaches 100°, it indicates slight feverishness. A morning temperature of 101° or 102°, to 103° in the evening, may be termed moderate fever; above 103° morning, and 104° evening, high fever.

THE PULSE.—From the temperature we pass naturally to the pulse. The latter indicates the rate of the engine, so to speak, as the former gauges the heat of the boiler or the amount of the fuel consumed. The pulse is the beat or impulse of the blood as driven by the heart's action against the walls of an artery; and we generally refer to the beat felt in what is known as the *radial artery*, as it passes over the front of the wrist immediately within its outer border. There is no such precise normal rate of pulse, as is generally supposed. Seventy-two beats in the minute is often stated to be the normal rate; but it is by no means so restricted as that. It varies greatly not only according to the

THE RATE OF THE PULSE. 31

amount of exercise we are taking at the time, but according to whether we are lying, sitting, or in the erect posture. It is the slower the more the body is at rest; it is quicker even after taking food. During sleep it is slower and more regular than at any other time. Suppose, then, you count the healthy pulse in the evening, the person being at rest, you will find it beat about sixty in the minute, which is the rate of a pendulum ticking once in a second. But in the forenoon, while engaged at one's ordinary duties, it will be ten or fifteen beats higher. It is quicker in children than in adults; in women than in men.

I would advise you to endeavour to acquire the rhythm of a clock ticking sixty in the minute and in that way you will have as a basis the beat of a rather slow pulse. Double that, and you will have a very quick pulse—120. But no one depends now on any natural power to estimate the rate of the pulse. It is invariably counted from a watch, and from one having a smaller second hand dial plate. To count a pulse is not a difficult thing. First find it where I stated, immediately within the prominent tendon of the thumb, and placing two fingers upon it, get a general idea of its rhythm. Then look at the moment hand of your watch, and begin counting with the first beat of the pulse, *after the second hand has passed* say the number 60, and continue counting *till the instant it has again arrived at that point*. If you are careful to do this exactly and count during a complete minute, you will be able to take a pulse with perfect accuracy. I am not, of course, including a very irregular or an intermittent pulse (in which every other beat is lost), or one of extreme rapidity; these being exceptional conditions.

Hitherto I have spoken of what a nurse can readily do; we have been dealing with matters of fact: but when we pass to what are known as the *qualities* of a pulse, we enter upon quite debatable ground; we deal with what is more a question of opinion. When a doctor speaks of a hard or a soft pulse, he considers the degree of resistance to the pressure of his finger on the artery: he speaks of a full or a thin pulse, according to his idea of the volume of blood passing along the vessel. You will also hear such expressions as a bounding pulse, or a wiry pulse, &c. Now if such questions are of any consequence to you, it can only be in one connection, viz., the administration of alcoholic stimulants. But I am one of those who think that in that connection it does concern you to acquire some knowledge of the quality of a pulse. It is admitted to be, in so far as it indicates the condition of the heart, the most important guide to the administration of stimulants. And when we consider that the indications for their increase or diminution may occur at any time, may occur during the night when only the nurse is present, we need not say how important it is to have one, who, within well defined limits, may be trusted to use her discretion in their administration. But you are not to act on what I am going to say, unless with express permission; I only wish you to know one or two points upon which authorities are quite agreed.

1. It is not a rapid pulse, so much as a soft, weak or easily pressed-out pulse, that indicates the necessity for stimulants.

2. If the pulse become slower and fuller, stimulants are doing good.

3. If the pulse become quicker and the face flush, stimulants are doing harm. And leaving the pulse we may add :—

4. If on sitting up in bed there be a tendency to fainting, stimulants are indicated: so also if there be coldness of the extremities.

With the kind of stimulants or the general quantity you have nothing to do. What you have to do invariably, is,—1. To administer it at the hours stated; and 2. To measure carefully and give the quantity ordered for each dose. It is only under express instructions that you are to act according to your own discretion as indicated above.

RESPIRATION.—In connection with the temperature, and pulse, or independently of these, you may have to count the movements of respiration. You all know that by respiration we mean the act of drawing air into the lungs and again expelling it. What we call drawing in the breath is more correctly raising the ribs and lowering the diaphragm or midriff.* In

---

* The broad expanded muscle which forms a cross partition between the chest and the abdomen.

THE LUNGS AND RESPIRATION. 35

this way the cavity of the chest is enlarged, the lungs are forced to expand, and the air rushes in. Then on the walls of the chest contracting, and the diaphragm rising, the elastic tissue of the lungs contracts and the air is forced or breathed out. The passage for the air begins with the windpipe, which runs down the neck to the upper part of the chest. There it divides, just like the trunk of a tree, into two great branches, one to each lung. Each of these again quickly divides and sub-divides as the branches of a tree do. After becoming very small they terminate in vesicles called air-cells, over which the fine bloodvessels of the lung run; and through which the blood in these vessels is changed by the air in the cells, from dark blue venous blood to bright red arterial blood. It is inflammation of these air-branches or *bronchi* which we call "*bronchitis*": it is from some part of their course that the spit or expectoration is brought up, and it is to effect this that we cough: it is, among other things, to listen how the air is making its way along these passages, that the physician uses his stethoscope. Most of these questions, however, we shall consider in detail at a future lecture.

To return to the taking of the respiration. You must always remember that this respiratory movement is partly under the control of the will; and that whenever we think of our breathing we necessarily exercise to some extent this control. For natural breathing must be unconscious breathing. You must endeavour then always to count the respirations unobserved. This you can do the more readily, that you can do it by sight alone. In the male, respiration is chiefly abdominal, or more correctly, diaphragmatic, *i.e.*, affected by the rise and fall of the diaphragm. In this way there is a movement carried to the abdominal wall by which we can easily observe and accurately count the number of respirations. In the female it is chiefly costal, *i.e*, affected by the rise and fall of the ribs. You can easily therefore count the respirations by sight alone, and when the patient thinks you are doing something else; for example, continuing to count his pulse. If possible count it during sleep, when it is always slowest and most regular; and at least let the patient be lying still and undisturbed. In health the rate of respiration varies from 12 to 18 or 20 in the minute, being higher in women and children. When it rises above 20 it is suspicious.

Then there is the character of the respiration. It may be frequent or slow; easy or laborious. It may be slow and yet laborious, as in severe chronic bronchitis. It may be frequent and shallow from the pain which it occasions, as in certain diseases of both chest and abdomen. Any occurrence of this kind should be carefully noted. So also any obstruction to the breathing about the throat, indicated by a peculiar harsh blowing sound, which conveys to one's mind, without any description, its true cause.

I conclude by giving you two words which you need never use, but the meaning of which you should understand—*dyspnœa* and *orthopnœa*. The first means difficult breathing, whether from obstruction or from the respiration being rapid; the second means inability to lie down in bed on account of the difficulty in breathing.

QUESTIONS ON LECTURE II.

1. Why is the temperature of the body a valuable guide to diagnosis?

2. Explain the principles on which a clinical thermometer is constructed.

3. At what time would you ordinarily take the temperature, and why?

4. What is the normal temperature of the body?

5. How would you take the temperature in the axilla? and give your reasons for so doing.

6. How would you take the pulse at the wrist?

7. What was said about the pulse in relation to stimulants?

8. What is the best mode of counting the respiration, and why?

9. Mention one or two kinds of abnormal respiration.

LECTURE III.

Cough—Expectoration—Hæmoptysis—Hæmatemesis—
Ventilation—Food or Diet.

At the close of last lecture we referred to the observation of respiration in connection with that of temperature and pulse. To-day we begin with the observation of some symptoms connected specially with disease of the respiratory organs.

These are mainly two—Cough and Expectoration. To the physician they are both of great importance as indications of disease, but you have to do chiefly with the latter; and with regard to it you have chiefly to know that in all cases it must be kept for the doctor's inspection. In this respect it is like the record of the temperature. The cough, on the other hand, like the pulse, cannot be kept. Your report, therefore, on its characters must be founded on your own opinion; and I would like you to be able to form an opinion worth reporting.

COUGH.—A cough is a sudden expiration forced through the upper end of the windpipe from a sense of something to be dislodged there. It may only be a sense of something, or there may really be something. This fact furnishes us with a convenient and common division of coughs into *dry* and *moist*.

1. A dry cough. This is the form which is often called a hard cough, and sometimes a tickling cough. There is nothing about the windpipe to be brought up; the irritation is in the nerves of the part, and may be brought to them from the most distant parts of the lungs, or even beyond them. You must, therefore, be careful to note the cough whatever disease the patient is supposed to suffer from.

2. A moist cough. Often termed a soft cough. It is a cough with expectoration; the object being to expel the undue secretion from the windpipe or from the bronchial tubes. Besides these characters you will note also its

VARIETIES OF COUGH.   41.

severity, and its frequency generally or at some special period of the twenty-four hours. A cough is often most severe during the night; and sometimes, as in hooping-cough, its diminution in severity and frequency then, is the first indication of improvement (West). In hooping-cough there is, of course, the characteristic crowing noise or "whoop," which gives the disease its name; and anything like that, or any peculiarity in the sound of the cough, you would note and report.

If a patient is coughing ineffectually to expel the defluxion, and the general sense of discomfort is not great, you may tell him with advantage to control, if possible, the cough, and the defluxion will itself make its way into the throat and be then coughed up easily. But if the feeling of obstruction is great he cannot resist the impulse to cough. Again, some forms of the dry tickling cough may be controlled; for example, "the cough of habit," as it is called; and it is quite your duty to remind the patient now and then to control it somewhat.

THE EXPECTORATION: the *sputum* or spit

(pl., *sputa*). It is the undue amount of secretion or defluxion discharged from the air-tubes. It varies much in character as well as in amount, and as I have said, should always be kept for the doctor's inspection. This is usually done by collecting it in an earthenware spittoon. Three varieties may be mentioned.

1. Mucous spit. It consists almost entirely of mucus, and is fluid, clear and transparent, with few air-bells. It indicates the least departure from health.

2. Muco-purulent spit. As its name implies it combines the characters of the other two. It is frothy owing to the mucous portion being intimately mixed with air; the purulent and heavier portion falls towards the bottom of the dish. It is the most common variety.

3. Purulent spit. This is all or in great part pure pus. It indicates an advanced or chronic stage of disease, though the particular disease may be comparatively trifling. Blood in the sputum must never be overlooked. It may appear as spots or streaks; or it may be so intimately mixed with the spit as to lose its

VARIETIES OF EXPECTORATION. 43

characteristic colour and give to the expectoration generally a brownish or rusty tinge.

When blood alone is expectorated, *i.e.*, brought up from the chest, we call it *hæmoptysis*. It is usually coughed up; is of a bright red colour, fluid and frothy. If blood comes from the stomach it will be darker and not frothy; possibly with some clots and mixed with food. If it has been lying for a time in the stomach it may closely resemble coffee grounds. This form of hæmorrhage is called *hæmatemesis*. It is of little consequence for you to remember the names of these two kinds of bleeding: it is more to the point to remember that anything of the kind should invariably be noted by you, and the ejected matters kept for the doctor's inspection. Either form of hæmorrhage, if alarming, may be treated by you in an emergency, by applying a folded towel, wrung out of ice-cold water, to the chest or pit of the stomach. The patient should be kept quiet and in the recumbent position, and medical assistance obtained.

In all chest affections where a physical examination, as it is termed, has to be made (an examination by *percussing* or striking the chest, or by means of the stethoscope, &c.), it is your duty to assist in many ways. See that the patient lies evenly on his back with the head rather low. Loosen the night dress at the neck, if necessary, and arrange it or hold it in such a way as you suppose the physician wishes in the particular case. Place the towel which you will have in your hand over the patient's side, so as to be between him and the physician, and yet so as not to interfere with the examination.

VENTILATION.—From the symptoms of disease of the lungs, we may pass on to the consideration of food for the lungs and how to obtain it; in other words, fresh air and ventilation.

Fresh air is one of those good things of which we cannot have too much. And there is plenty of it to be had. It completely envelopes our world. It rises above it for many miles, and goes down, too, into the depths of the sea. It is the life of every thing that lives. This is the food that the lungs must have, and as it is your duty to see that the food is good, I must tell you something about it.

Air may be regarded as invisible, without colour, taste, or smell: we might almost doubt its existence did it not remind us of its presence in the gentle breeze, and sometimes of its awful power in the stormy tempest. We know then that it exists; but what is its nature? It is not a simple body; it is not one of the elements, as the ancients supposed, but a compound body. It consists mainly of two elements, *oxygen* and *nitrogen*. Oxygen is a gas, without colour, taste, or smell. It sustains animal life, and supports combustion, *i.e.*, enables fuel to burn. It is the life-giving principle of the air, although there is only one part of it to four of nitrogen. Nitrogen is also devoid of colour, taste, or smell. It extinguishes life and light. It modifies the vital properties of the oxygen, or, as has been said, " it dilutes the oxygen as water does wine or spirits." These two elements form almost the whole bulk of the atmosphere; but there is a third body, which, although there is only a trace of it in the air as a whole, is so poisonous in itself, and so readily increases in circumstances that concern us very directly, that we must give it our most careful attention. It is called *carbonic acid*.

Carbonic acid is a compound body devoid of colour, but with a slight smell and a sourish taste. It extinguishes light, and if breathed undiluted, destroys life instantly. Pure air contains, as I have said, only a trace of it. There is rather less than one part of carbonic acid in 2000 parts of the atmosphere as a whole. If there is 1 part in 1000 of air, say, in a room, we feel it to be distinctly stuffy and close. You will almost guess already why it so directly demands our attention. We cannot remain in a room without increasing the quantity of this poisonous gas. With every expiration we give out at once impure air,—air so far unfit to be breathed by our own selves again. Hence the necessity for ventilation. But besides breathing out this poisonous gas, we continually remove some of the life-giving oxygen; the carbonic acid expired being formed by the combination of oxygen with the carbon of our bodies. Thus a double injury, so to speak, is being done to the air when we breathe it. But you may ask why, if every human being and all the lower animals are doing this, does not the whole external atmosphere at last become unfit for breathing? It is just because plants do exactly the opposite. They take in carbonic acid and give out oxygen. The vegetable kingdom lives on what the animal kingdom would die on, and *vice versa*. But there is one qualification of this law which you must remember. *During the night* plants, like animals, give out carbonic acid. Not to such an extent as to undo the important office they have fulfilled during the day time, but quite sufficiently to make it necessary for you to learn this practical lesson—*never allow flowers to remain in a sick room during the night.*

You now understand why fresh air is so essential, and how foul air continually forms: you understand the necessity for ventilation. Here is Dr. Parke's definition of it:—" Proper ventilation is clean air displacing foul air constantly and steadily, without chilling the patient." You should commit this to memory:

it is your whole duty in the matter. You have the disease and the remedy, with the mode of administering it, in a single sentence. We shall now see how proper ventilation can be obtained.

First let us look at one or two general principles. The inlet for the fresh air should, theoretically, be at the floor of the room. Theoretically, because the natural direction of air as it becomes warm, and, in the case of an occupied room, impure, is from below upwards. But practically such an inlet chills our feet, and it is better to be at a height quite above that of any one walking about the room; or it may even be near the ceiling, where if thrown across the room the cooler air will gradually descend. The outlet, if there is no heating apparatus in the ward or room, should be at the highest part of the room, whither the heated and impure air has gone. If there is a fire on, then the air will make its way by the fireplace up the chimney, or it may be allowed to escape by a ventilator into the chimney. Remember that artificial heat always makes ventilation much more certain and constant.

I have spoken about warm air and impure air, but you must not fall into the common mistake of supposing that there is any essential connection between these two conditions. Warm air may be perfectly pure, and *vice versa*. Warm air and impure air are only commonly associated because they are both a result of the air of a room being breathed.

Another practical point to attend to is this. Judge of the state of the air in a room immediately on coming in from the pure outside atmosphere. After remaining a few minutes in a room, you cannot detect the closeness directly by the senses; but you may very soon do so indirectly by getting a most disagreeable headache.

From what I have said you will understand the principles on which, for example, the wards of a hospital are ventilated. Our wards here are constructed on such principles, and you have simply to put them into practice. But we come now to a very different thing: what may be a very difficult thing to effect— the ventilation of an ordinary sick-room. When a hospital or a dwelling-house is to be built, the architect has simply to select the plan of ventilating which he thinks best; and as regards details he has a wide choice. When we enter a sick-room we have to make the best of what already is; and there is usually but little to choose from.

Before giving you two methods of almost universal application in private nursing, I wish you to note the following general rules. They apply more particularly to a case of some severity, and which will likely be of considerable duration.

Choose the largest and airiest room in the house; the sunny side if possible. In a large room the air does not require to be renewed so often, and the liability to draughts is thus lessened.

Remove any obstruction that may be about the fireplace, and have a fire on. I say nothing about a bedroom without a fireplace—that is simply out of the question altogether. Should the weather be warm the fire can be kept low. Even a lighted lamp in the grate is of service; anything that will heat the air and make it pass up the chimney, for then fresh air *will* find its way in somehow.

Never light the gas of a room merely as a means of heating it. Any slight rise in the temperature of the apartment is more than counterbalanced by the amount of oxygen consumed and carbonic acid formed in the process; besides other impurities.

Except in special cases allow plenty of sunlight into the room. Sunlight and pure air work hand in hand. The patient should not face the window; if he does so, let the light be lessened when he feels it irksome. In exceptional cases it may be necessary to keep the room specially dark. For this purpose a dark green window blind is best. The bed should be away from the wall on all sides, to admit of free access to the patient; and from what I have said you will understand that if it be between the door and the fire, or between the window and the fire, you will need to take precautions against a draught.

Have no curtains about the bed, and remove everything from the room not actually required. Keep all medicine bottles, pill-boxes, and such like, out of the patient's sight. Other questions relating to the management of the sick-room will be considered by and bye when we come to speak of the prevention of infection.

Returning now to ventilation, we have still to consider some special methods of ventilating a room that you can adopt in any circumstances. These are really very few. I shall give you only two.

Get a piece of wood, about 4 inches broad, and of the same length as the breadth of the window sash frame. Raise the lower sash so that the piece of wood may be fitted into the space left. In this way a current of air will be admitted between the upper and lower sash, at such a height from the floor as will not readily cause any draught. This now well-known method was recommended first by Mr. Hinckes Bird; he called it "costless ventilation."

The second method, however, which I have

VENTILATION OF WARD.

to mention, costs less ; we only require to have windows and doors in the house. Cover the patient well with the bed-clothes, perhaps putting on an extra blanket and drawing it up over the mouth. Then open the windows freely, top and bottom, and the doors too, unless there be any special reason to the contrary, such as an infectious disease. Close them again in five or ten minutes, but continue the extra covering on the patient till the room returns to its proper temperature, and then let him be as before. With such precautions, he will not catch cold. The temperature of the sick-room should be in most cases from 60° to 65° Fah.

In hospital it is a good rule always to have some of the windows on one side of the ward, preferably the windward side, drawn an inch or two from the top. You have thus a steady and not a fitful supply of fresh air, and so you lessen the risk of draughts. They may, of course, sometimes be opened wider, according to circumstances, but they should constantly be open to some extent. The rule has always been to dread even a whiff of the fresh night air entering the sick-room, and it is not surprising that some are now going too far towards the opposite extreme. But it is certainly true that one almost never catches cold in bed; and that an amount of fresh air which the patient just feels playing across his face will seldom do him any harm.

I find I have time yet to enter upon a new subject, not food for the lungs, but food in the ordinary acceptation of the term. We have therefore to consider now :—

FOOD or DIET.—Diet is food viewed collectively; a patient's diet usually means his food administered on some regular principle by the doctor's directions. Health demands that our food proper should be, like our food for the lungs, good. The demand, unfortunately, is too often unheeded or misinterpreted. I think every person in health instinctively recognises the kind of food that is best for him, not merely generally, but for him specially. But the humblest live under conditions now-a-days that readily tempt to food and to drink too that should be forbidden; and when disease in one or other form is induced, a par-

CLASSIFICATION OF FOOD.

ticular diet requires to be laid down, which it becomes your duty to see carried out.

We all realise the necessity of food in some form. Every step we take, the slightest movements of our body, are associated with a certain amount of loss of tissue which must be replaced. Our bodies, too, have constantly to withstand the contact with the colder atmosphere, which continually tends to lower the essential temperature of health. Food makes up for the waste resulting from this wear and tear, and supplies the heat that is required to keep our bodies at the normal temperature. Viewed, therefore, as fulfilling these two conditions, it is commonly divided into—1, Tissue-forming, and 2, Heat-producing, some parts of our food being devoted more to the one object, and other parts to the other.

Food considered in itself has been classified in many ways. A common one, and employing simple terms, is into the following four groups:—1. *The Albuminous* or *Fibrinous*. This class includes the constituents of our food that are chiefly tissue-forming, *i.e.*, forming muscles and supplying generally what is lost by bodily wear and tear. It is represented in meat by the lean; in an egg by the albumen or white; in bread by what is called gluten; and so on. 2. *The Oleaginous or Fatty.* This class includes foods which are principally heat-producing, viz., animal fats and vegetable oils. Such foods are instinctively taken in large quantities in northern regions; and we find that cod liver oil, for example, is better borne in winter than in summer. 3. *The Saccharine or Sugary.* This includes not merely all forms of sugar, but the closely-allied starchy constituents of food, which are very readily changed into sugar. They form the greater part of vegetable food, *e.g.*, fruits, grains, roots, &c. This class, like the oleaginous, is chiefly heat-producing. 4. *The Aqueous or Watery.* This is hardly entitled to be called a class. It includes the water that is to be found to some extent in all food products, along with various salts held in solution.

You will not forget these four well-recognised groups; our food collectively must be drawn from every one of them. We could not live on any one alone, however great

MILK AS FOOD.

a variety of articles of diet we might select from it. We might try, for example, to live on the lean of meat, the white of egg, gluten bread, and cheese, which all belong to class 1, but however daintily and variedly cooked they would not long sustain life. It is interesting on the other hand to know that some kinds of diet which appear to be of the simplest, as they are indeed of the lightest character, really contain all the four essential principles. You have heard it said, I daresay, that one may live on milk alone. It is possible, though not just the kind of food one would select who was engaged in active work. In it the fibrinous principles are represented by the casein of milk, which we use in the form of cheese; the oleaginous or fatty, by the cream or butter; the saccharine, by the sugar of milk, which can easily be separated from it; and then there is naturally, not to speak of artificially, a considerable proportion of water, with some salts in solution.

We shall say something at next lecture on the digestion of food.

QUESTIONS ON LECTURE III.

1. Describe the different kinds of cough mentioned.

2. What practical points are referred to in connection with the different kinds?

3. What are the three principal varieties of sputa?

4. Give the general distinguishing features of blood brought up from the lungs and the stomach respectively.

5. Of what gases does the air consist, and in what proportions? Mention some of the characteristics of each.

6. Why is ventilation necessary? Define proper ventilation.

7. Describe two different methods of ventilating a sick-room.

8. What distinct objects does food fulfil in the animal economy, and what classification has this led to?

9. Give another classification of food.

LECTURE IV.

THE DIGESTION OF FOOD—PRACTICAL LESSONS TO BE DRAWN—DIGESTIBILITY OF DIFFERENT FORMS OF DIET—THE COOKING OF FOOD—THE ADMINISTRATION OF FOOD.

By the digestion of food we mean its conversion into a state in which it is fitted to be taken up or *assimilated* by the system. When you think on these distinct food principles which I mentioned at last lecture, you will be prepared to hear that digestion is not after all such a simple thing as you may have supposed. In health, it is apparently a simple thing and we do not even think about it, but in disease it is very different. Then a great many questions are forced upon the attention of both patient and attendant; and I wish to-day to consider shortly such points connected with digestion as will enable you to understand why this should be so; and why you are directed to do, or should do, certain things, in the matter of a patient's diet.

Digestion may be said to begin in the mouth. There the food is (1) Broken up by the teeth, and (2) Reduced to a soft pulp by the saliva, as mere water cannot possibly do, so as to make it easily swallowed. Besides this the food is acted on chemically by the saliva, in such a way that its starchy constituents become changed into sugar; an alteration which, you will remember, they readily undergo. The albuminous and oleaginous elements are not acted upon chemically by the saliva.

When the food reaches the stomach it comes under the influence of the *gastric juice,* a fluid consisting mainly of *pepsine* and an acid resembling hydrochloric acid. This fluid continues the changes already begun on the food as a whole, reducing it all to a pulp, and completely dissolving some parts of it.

Immediately on the food entering the stomach, its walls on all sides begin to pour out gastric juice; and, as we can understand, those portions of food lying next the walls are acted upon first. But now a curious muscular movement of the stomach commences by which these portions of the food first digested are thrown inwards, while fresh portions are thereby brought into contact with the walls, to be again driven inwards and replaced by less digested parts.

Another remarkable power which the stomach has, is that of moving or sending on parts of the food as soon as they become sufficiently digested and retaining the rest— a process of selection as essential as it is wonderful, because some portions of our food are digested much more slowly than others.

The fatty ingredients of our food are not, properly speaking, digested in the stomach. They merely undergo a mechanical division into much smaller particles, and are then carried into the first or highest part of the small intestine, where their digestion really takes place through the action of the secretion from the liver and pancreas.

As to the saccharine elements, the gastric juice has rather a secondary action on them, the saliva, as already stated, being the first and probably the main agent in their digestion. Fluids are directly absorbed by the stomach.

So much for general principles. I would just add that vegetable food is as a rule difficult of digestion, particularly what are called the cell walls of vegetable structures, which may resist digestion altogether.

Such is a very partial outline of the process of digestion. I would commend to your consideration the further study of that and other similar questions, which you will find fully yet simply explained in several well written popular text-books on physiology. My object has been to mention little more than such facts as will furnish a lesson of direct practical value to you; and these facts we shall now consider in the order in which they have been stated.

First, then, you must not forget the important part that mastication fulfils. If imperfectly performed it may itself lead to indigestion, as the great French physician Trousseau tells us. Should this result from carelessness, you may advise the patient accordingly; if from the necessity that old age imposes, then the toothless gums must be aided by the administration of softer and pulpier food. But whether the food can be well chewed or not, time should be given to admit of it being acted upon by the saliva, particularly in the case of vegetable products which consist largely of starchy principles. You will see, therefore, the impropriety of the invalid taking his bread *in* his beef tea or chicken soup, if it leads him to avoid chewing it carefully and so bringing it at the same time under the influence of the saliva. He had much better take the bread separately.

In some forms of indigestion the physician administers pepsine and other similar natural secretions which are obtained from such animals as the calf or pig; but this I only notice in passing. (See "Peptonised Foods" in Appendix.)

The muscular movement of the stomach walls, which the presence of food occasions, must always be taken into account in any structural disease of that organ. You can understand why, for example, in a case of ulcer of the stomach, you are directed to give food, not only which is very light and digestible, but also in very small quantities at a time: less movement, less disturbance is set up.

To come now to the next steps in the process of digestion to which we referred. In giving food often we must avoid the danger of giving it too often, which we may readily do if the quantity is not very small, and the food of the lightest character. We may give food before the last meal is digested, imposing needlessly on the stomach the exercise of that power of selection to which I directed your attention. Even in a healthy person this may cause temporary indigestion.

As to the digestion of fatty principles, you should always, unless specially directed otherwise, give cod-liver oil immediately *after* food. It is certainly more easily borne by the stomach then, probably because it undergoes the necessary mechanical subdivision more thoroughly with the rest of the food, after which it becomes naturally acted upon by the secretion from the liver and pancreas.

The last point, the comparative indigestibility of the stronger vegetables, is one which will rarely concern you as nurses. You will probably never be directed to give, for example, "Scotch broth" to a patient with weak digestion; at the same time, to know what vegetables *may* be given, what food generally may be given, will sometimes be of great value to you, at least in private nursing. This we are now going to consider.

I need not remind you that a patient's diet is a question for the medical attendant alone; so that although I am going to tell you something about different kinds of food as articles of diet, it will be, like much else I shall tell you, only as general information which in particular cases may be of service to you.

In any form of disease which has induced general debility the stomach is necessarily involved as well. It loses its *tone*, as we say. This itself, however, may be the particular disease: what is called *atonic dyspepsia*. Whether it be so, or depending on a general loss of strength such as occurs in all acute diseases, we require to begin with light food; sometimes the very lightest we can think of. Beginning, then, with the lightest articles of diet, we mention first, whey, milk and soda water, and milk alone. Whey is what is left from milk when all the *casein*, the albuminous principle, is separated from it as curds. It is lighter, but of course much less nutritious than milk. Milk and soda water is lighter than milk in proportion to the amount of the latter added, and so much the less nutritious. Two parts of milk and one part of soda water is a usual proportion. If soda water is not to be had, about 10 grains of bicarbonate of soda dissolved in as much water as you will add to a pint of milk is a good substitute. Milk itself comes next.

Such forms of food you will often be directed to give; but more than that, you will be told probably to give them in small quantities at a time. You may find it necessary to give only a dessertspoonful, say, of milk and soda water every quarter of an hour, and even that the stomach may not retain. In such circumstances, keep the patient still, with the head rather low, and add a little ice to the milk, or place a small piece in the patient's mouth. Such plans as these you may have to adopt on

LIGHT DIET.

your own responsibility till you get further instructions from the doctor. Once the stomach's scruples are overcome, you may cautiously increase the amount you give at a time, and lessen the proportion of soda water in the milk.

From this the patient may pass to chicken soup or beef tea, with which perhaps a little toasted bread or water-biscuit is given, taking the precaution already referred to. Chicken soup is often preferred when cooled to a jelly, and of this a teaspoonful at a time may be enough. Beef tea or a little essence of beef may sometimes be given; *iced* in some cases with advantage. Of the two, chicken soup is lighter and generally more palatable.

The next stage, as we may call it, includes chicken, sweetbread, or the more homely dish of tripe, if the patient can take it; boiled white fish such as haddocks, whiting, turbot, etc., and any light farinaceous pudding or custard. When the patient can take these dishes it is time to think what vegetables may be added. Cauliflower is probably the lightest, but asparagus, spinach, and generally the more tender vegetables may be tried.

We come next to ordinary diet. Here we need only say that mutton (boiled) is the lightest form of butcher meat.

We have now to consider lastly what should be avoided by the dyspeptic patient. There is no precise rule in this respect, but the following may be set down as objectionable—salted meats, pork, game, pastry, cheese, nuts, shellfish, and all raw fruits, except grapes, oranges, and strawberries.

We pass now to a part of our subject that I take up with some hesitancy :—

THE COOKING OF FOOD.—With its practical details you must be more familiar than I am; still there are some general considerations to which I may profitably direct your attention. There can be no doubt that the manner in which food is cooked and served bears very directly on its digestibility and the readiness with which the patient will take it. And these are all important considerations. It is with these objects that we cook at all. It increases the your own responsibility till you get further instructions from the doctor. Once the stomach's scruples are overcome, you may cautiously increase the amount you give at a time, and lessen the proportion of soda water in the milk.

From this the patient may pass to chicken soup or beef tea, with which perhaps a little toasted bread or water-biscuit is given, taking the precaution already referred to. Chicken soup is often preferred when cooled to a jelly, and of this a teaspoonful at a time may be enough. Beef tea or a little essence of beef may sometimes be given; *iced* in some cases with advantage. Of the two, chicken soup is lighter and generally more palatable.

The next stage, as we may call it, includes chicken, sweetbread, or the more homely dish of tripe, if the patient can take it; boiled white fish such as haddocks, whiting, turbot, etc., and any light farinaceous pudding or custard. When the patient can take these dishes it is time to think what vegetables may be added. Cauliflower is probably the lightest, but asparagus, spinach, and generally the more tender vegetables may be tried.

We come next to ordinary diet. Here we need only say that mutton (boiled) is the lightest form of butcher meat.

We have now to consider lastly what should be avoided by the dyspeptic patient. There is no precise rule in this respect, but the following may be set down as objectionable—salted meats, pork, game, pastry, cheese, nuts, shellfish, and all raw fruits, except grapes, oranges, and strawberries.

We pass now to a part of our subject that I take up with some hesitancy :—

THE COOKING OF FOOD.—With its practical details you must be more familiar than I am; still there are some general considerations to which I may profitably direct your attention. There can be no doubt that the manner in which food is cooked and served bears very directly on its digestibility and the readiness with which the patient will take it. And these are all important considerations. It is with these objects that we cook at all. It increases the digestibility of the food and imparts a new flavour to it, depending on some chemical changes not well understood. I need not apologise, therefore, for directing your attention to such questions.

Of the different methods of cooking, it is generally considered that boiling is the lightest and simplest; and it is the most economical. Water being the medium in which the food is cooked, the heat is never so excessive as to cause it in that way to be overdone; nor will the water itself, as a medium, lead to those chemical changes which occur so readily in some other forms of cooking, rendering the food quite unsuitable for the ordinary patient. In cooking meat in this way, you know that it should be put first into boiling water—a temperature of 212° Fah. You do this that the boiling water may coagulate the albumen on the surface of the meat, and so close up the pores there that the juices of the meat cannot escape. Having done so, the temperature of the water should be let fall to 160° or 170° Fah. If, on the other hand, you are making beef tea or soup, you cut the meat into small pieces, place it in cold water and gradually raise the temperature.

Broiling is probably as light a method of cooking, but it is not so easy to do it well. The risk of overdoing it, and so impairing the nutritive qualities of the food, is greater. In a rough way, it is likely to have been the earliest form of cooking by placing seeds or flesh among the hot ashes of the fire. To do it properly, you require a clear, uniform charcoal fire, and the gridiron itself should be heated first; the object being to coagulate as quickly as possible all the albumen on the surface of the meat. It should always be done *over* the fire and not *in front* of it, for then the draught coming towards the fire will necessarily cool one side of the meat.

Roasting comes next in order of lightness, and of it I do not need to say anything.

For invalids, stewing, baking, and frying are most objectionable methods of cooking, particularly the last, as I have said, on account of the fatty acids that are formed in the process.

With regard to the cooking of vegetables, I

will venture to say, though with some fear of contradiction, that any means employed by which their colour is preserved, whatever these means be, render them so much the less digestible. The colouring matter itself is said to resist digestion greatly, and certainly its preservation indicates that the walls of the starch cells are not burst in the process of cooking, as they ought to be, and their contents therefore not acted on so as to render them more digestible, as proper cooking always does. The stronger vegetables, such as cabbage, greens, carrots, etc., cannot be boiled too long.

We come now to a part of our subject that is peculiarly your own :—

THE ADMINISTRATION OF FOOD.—It is as important a matter as any that we have considered. The diet may be wisely laid down, the food well cooked, and yet the neglect of some apparently little detail in the way in which it is presented to the patient may undo all that has preceded. Hence the rule that whatever you are going to give to a patient should be made as inviting as possible. For this object there is surely nothing so imperatively necessary as that everything should be scrupulously clean. Every patient is entitled to that at least; but in private nursing you will find that, in addition, little points of neatness or other similar questions of detail may be essential to the proper enjoyment of the meal. These must be left to your own good sense, and I only intend to mention some well-recognised rules for your general guidance.

Remembering, then, what I have just said, you will see that the feeding cup and all vessels used for food or medicine are kept thoroughly clean. It is a good plan to have a second feeding cup which is to be used only for giving medicines. You will find a bent glass tube very useful. It has been often remarked that a patient will take a little fluid nourishment through the tube when he will not have the feeding cup, and yet must be fed in some such way. After use the tube should be held under the tap in order to be thoroughly washed out. It should then be kept lying in fresh water.

There are one or two little matters that it

may be necessary, in some cases, to attend to before the patient can be induced to take his food. If there is great weakness, and, particularly, if it is a case of fever, the tongue is likely to be foul and dry, and the mouth and teeth coated with an offensive deposit called *sordes*. It consists of waste materials from the mucous membrane of the mouth, and other products, the result of disordered secretion. Before the patient can be induced to taste food it may be necessary to have this cleaned away. A good wash for the mouth is formed by adding half an ounce of Condy's Fluid to a pint of water. "To cleanse the teeth and gums, cut a small slice of lemon and rub it gently but firmly over the teeth, tongue, and lips. Then with a little pure water and a charpie brush rapidly wash over the same." * Another method I have tried is by means of a soft tooth brush, to cleanse the mouth and

---

* "This," says Miss Florence Lees in her Handbook for Hospital Sisters, "was the method taught me by the Sœurs Augustines in the Hôtel Dieu, Paris. The 'charpie brushes' were made by tying a small bunch of charpie to a piece of stick."

gums with a little glycerine of borax, to which a few grains of citric acid have been added. You could get from the druggist one ounce of glycerine of borax with ten grains of citric acid dissolved in it. Besides this, it is well to wet the lips and tongue of a fevered patient frequently with simple water perhaps, or some acid solution such as lime juice. A small piece of ice in the mouth occasionally is always grateful and always safe.

If the patient is in a state of semi-delirium or coma, endeavour to rouse him somewhat before giving him his food. Sometimes merely putting the spoon to his mouth is enough; at other times you will require to get it well to the back of the tongue. In such cases watch carefully to see that the liquid is swallowed before attempting to give a second spoonful. It may sometimes be difficult for you to know whether or not a patient should be roused in this way to take food, because he may be sleeping naturally. If, in any special case, you feel a difficulty in this respect, you must ask for special instructions. It is, however, accepted as a sound general rule that, if a patient is sleeping naturally, he is not to be awakened for either food or stimulants.

I conclude with a few general principles regarding the administration of food in cases of pronounced weakness. I have always found that any one of much experience in the care of the sick or who has passed through a severe or prolonged illness herself, has thoroughly endorsed Miss Nightingale's remark that in such circumstances *the patient should never be asked beforehand what he will have.** Prepare some suitable article of diet as best you can and set it before him in as inviting a way as possible. Let the patient have quietness when at meals; as a rule he is better to be alone. It is well, if possible, that he should see no food but his own.

Do not give the patient more at one time than you think he will likely finish. A large quantity suggests defeat before the attack has begun. Should anything be left do not let it

---

* This, of course, only applies to actual illness in which the appetite is capricious, or, it may be, quite gone. It is altogether different when convalescence has begun: then the patient takes a practical interest in his meals.

remain by his side. All food should be out of sight, and out of smell too, if possible, when it is being cooked. Of course all these rules cannot be closely and invariably followed in hospital, but you should secure such conditions as far as practicable, if the necessities of the case demand it. In private nursing the patient will be more accustomed to, and will more readily look for, these little attentions; and in such circumstances they can easily be carried out.

Then I would impress upon you the importance, the necessity of punctuality, in the serving of meals. A person in health generally expects punctuality in that respect, in whatever else he may be remiss: in disease you must be punctual for him. But even in disease there may be one particular hour at which he feels he could relish a little food; so never let that opportunity escape you. Keep to the same hour every day, or judiciously train your patient, should that be necessary, to keep to it.

Lastly, acquire the habit of observing with the same exactness how much the patient has taken. In no case are vague statements of any use; in some cases the precise quantity given must be noted just as carefully as the amount of medicine or stimulants which has been administered.

QUESTIONS ON LECTURE IV.

1. What changes does the food undergo—
    a. In the mouth?
    b. In the stomach?
    c. In the highest part of the small intestine?

2. What is the general dietetic treatment of ulcer of the stomach, and why?

3. Mention one or two of the lightest articles of diet, and the precautions you would take in extreme irritability of the stomach.

4. Name a few light dishes in what may be supposed to be their order of digestibility.

5. What kinds of food are to be avoided in cases of weakened digestion?

6. State what you know about boiling and frying as methods of cooking invalids' food.

7. What preliminary steps may be necessary, in some cases, to induce a patient to take food?

8. Mention the general principles referred to regarding the administration of food.

LECTURE V.

THE CARE OF SPECIAL DISEASES, MAINLY AS REGARDS DIET: DIARRHŒA — SCURVY — RICKETS—SCROFULA —RHEUMATISM—ANEURISM — DIABETES: GENERAL REFERENCE TO DISEASES OF THE KIDNEY.

WE begin to-day the consideration of diet in some special diseases, or, we might rather say, the consideration of some diseases in which a particular diet is required; for I shall in passing tell you something of the nature of the diseases as well as the part of their treatment which more directly concerns you.

DIARRHŒA.—We shall consider it first because it is a disorder affecting the intestinal canal itself; the very part of the body whose office it is to introduce the food to the system generally. Improper food, or an improper amount of food, is a common cause; but sudden chills, warm weather, and disorders of other parts of the body are examples of what also may occasion it. In this affection the lining membrane of the bowel is inflamed and irritable, or relaxed; such a condition requires a diet that will be *bland* and *astringent*. Milk, especially boiled milk, has to some degree these qualities naturally, and it is usually the basis of whatever diet is prescribed. The addition of equal parts, or perhaps a third, of lime water makes it more astringent. A little isinglass, dissolved first in water, and then added to the milk, becomes somewhat of a protective to the irritable bowel. A similar and very good preparation is one quart of milk mixed with the whites of three or four eggs beaten to a froth. Sometimes the milk may not agree, and it will be necessary to substitute simply the same quantity of water sweetened with a little fruit syrup of some kind.

A less common, but often most valuable kind of diet, particularly in the diarrhœa of children, is that of raw meat, a method of treatment that comes to us originally from Russia.

Its preparation will, of course, devolve upon you it is quite a simple matter. What you want is to leave all the shreddy fibrous tissue, and get only the soft pulp of the meat. This is done by taking a small piece of lean juicy meat, and scraping it with a knife in one direction. Each stroke of the knife will bring away on its edge some of the soft pulp, and this can be continued till nothing but shreddy indigestible fibre is left. A little salt may be added to the soft meat, which can then be spread on thin toast or biscuit. For a child of one year old it is usual to begin with one ounce in the day divided into three parts. If it is necessary to disguise it in some way a little jelly may be added.

I conclude the consideration of this disease with an important caution. Remember that in cases of diarrhœa you are not to give on your own responsibility that never-failing meal for invalids, a basin of beef-tea. In any such condition of the intestinal canal beef-tea is decidedly laxative. It is sometimes so in healthy children of one or two years of age.

We come next to a disease which is directly

caused by improper food, but which in its severer forms is almost never seen now; I mean:—

SCURVY.—We must not pass it by however, not only because it is sometimes seen in our wards, but because if you are engaged in district nursing you may see many cases of it in a milder form. It is a disease depending essentially on the use of improper food, and this may be the result of ignorance, indifference, or necessity. In its worst forms as it occurred in the old days, it was usually from the necessity imposed by war or long voyages in sailing ships, when it became impossible to obtain fresh supplies of food. Not so long ago, and nearer home, it has arisen from the necessity of poverty. Of the symptoms of the milder forms I need only mention a painful stiffness and hardness of the muscles, particularly of the lower limbs, and a discoloration of the skin in the neighbourhood of the ankles of a variable hue like the different stages of a bruise. This and also little irregular purplish spots or dots, which are sometimes seen scattered over the body, are caused by effusion of blood in varying amount underneath the skin. It is in that form, along with a general debility and a sallowness of complexion, that you will see it amongst those who take improper food from ignorance or carelessness — not the very poor necessarily, but those who cannot have, or will not take the trouble to have their food properly selected and cooked. A routine of tea, and soft "carried food," as it is called, will soon induce it. The remedy is fresh food, particularly vegetable food, freshly cooked. A dinner of a little good butcher meat or fish, with potatoes, cabbage, or other vegetable, will speedily cause it to disappear. Cresses, lettuce, etc., as a salad are very efficacious; and half a wine-glassful of lemon juice, with a little water, twice a day or so, is usually prescribed.

We pass now to the consideration of two diseases in which bad food is only one of several possible causes; and first:—

RICKETS.—Besides being fairly entitled to consideration here, it comes fittingly after the study of scurvy, and along with that of scrofula, which we shall take up next, because they are all diseases that to a greater or less degree are met with specially in district visitation or nursing, in which some of you I know are interested. This last fact is my reason also for saying more about their nature and symptoms than I would otherwise do.

Rickets, speaking generally, is indicated by curvature or other alteration in the shape and form of the bones. It is a disease peculiarly prevalent in large towns, and our own city shares, with a few others, the unenviable reputation of being one of its great centres. This circumstance has given my friend and colleague, Dr. Macewen, a larger field for that successful inroad upon its deformities which has made him so widely known.

The want of pure air, and of light and sunshine, is probably a cause to a greater degree than the want of proper food. The food supply of our West Highlands is generally speaking inferior to that of our inland towns, yet "although from most quarters in Scotland cases of distorted limbs have presented themselves for treatment (in our hospital) there has not been one from the West Highlands. The fresh air and the sea breezes appear to compensate for the lack of sufficient food." (Macewen). The water supply of our city has often and most undeservedly been blamed for its prevalence.

As regards symptoms, I need only refer to the most conspicuous, such as you would readily observe in district visitation. Before the long bones begin to bend there is usually some enlargement of their extremities, and as this is readily noticed at the wrist, and is often accompanied by flaccidity of the muscles, the idea of a double joint, whatever that really is, has found its way into the popular mind as a satisfactory explanation of the peculiarity.

But before this stage is reached, the child will have presented some indications of general debility, such as profuse sweating, particularly about the head and at night. And there is one early symptom that deserves your attention, viz., a general tenderness of the body. The child is clearly suffering from aching pains more or less over the whole body. It cries when touched, or at least if lifted incautiously; or perhaps when some particular limb is moved, or if it is put down to walk—a natural provision doubtless against the use of the readily yielding limbs. It is of great importance that this symptom should not be overlooked, and a friendly caution against forcing the child to walk will be timely and valuable advice. Should the mother think the child is simply peevish or petted and insist on it walking, the lower limbs will gradually bend under the weight of the child.

What is the cause of this bending? We may say simply that it is owing to diseased alterations in the growth or development of the bones. This growth, which occurs naturally in every young person, is not merely an increase in the size of the bones. There is that, of course, as there is that of all the structures of the body, but in addition the bones acquire those firm, hard, resisting qualities which characterise the bones of adults. Now in this disease the *form* of growth which is going on is unnatural. It is of such a kind that the earthy or inorganic matter which enters into the composition of bone, and gives it these qualities I have just mentioned, is greatly deficient, while the organic or living constituents are in excess. In health the proportions are just the opposite.

The alterations in the shape of the bones, though chiefly, are not exclusively found in those of the lower limbs. Curvature of the spine is not an uncommon result of rickets; so also that flattening of the sides of the ribs which forms what is called the "pigeon breast." In this case the movements of respiration have caused the softened ribs to yield inwards, and this again causes the breast bone to be projected forwards.

Although some slight bending of the bones of the leg may occur in children otherwise healthy and who have been brought up under the most favourable conditions, yet a neglect of ordinary sanitary laws is, as I have said, a great cause of rickets proper, and obviously the right treatment is to return to these neglected laws as quickly as possible. Good food, warm clothing, sunlight, and as much fresh air as can be obtained *without the child requiring to walk for it;* that is sound and safe advice to give to any family so afflicted.

Another disease common amongst the poor, though by no means exclusively confined to them, is:—

SCROFULA.—It is not a particular disease so much as a peculiar impaired state of the constitution which manifests itself in many forms of disease, often obstinate, too often quite intractable. As one of its most frequent indications are swellings and other changes in the glands of the neck which are apt to lead to ulceration and unsightly sores, it holds in the popular mind a by no means reputable position. But there is no opprobrium attached to it unless it is a shame to be weak in place of strong.

It is caused like rickets by conditions or circumstances which are opposed to the common laws of health. The treatment is much the same therefore as for the foregoing. Chemical food and cod liver oil have now become popular remedies for it, and, unlike many popular remedies, they are thoroughly appropriate.

The neglect of the ordinary laws of health is still a common evil which it should be

THE NURSING OF RHEUMATISM. 89

every one's duty, so far as possible, to correct. I have therefore discussed the foregoing disorders in a somewhat exceptional way. We shall now return to the consideration of your duties as nurses of the sick in hospital.

RHEUMATISM.—There is little to be said about diet in this affection, and it is more as a connecting link than from any special importance attaching to it, that I make the remark that we usually avoid giving animal food in this disease. The great point in the care of rheumatism, I mean particularly acute rheumatism (in which besides the pain there is high fever), is the avoidance of anything that will chill the patient. To emphasise this, one is almost justified in saying that here *warm* air is more important than fresh air. The least exposure to cold may greatly aggravate the disease. If details are left to you and the case is at all severe, you should see that the patient lies between blankets and that he wears a flannel night dress. One, or more likely several of his joints will be swollen and painful, and for that you may be ordered to apply fomentations to the inflamed parts, or perhaps a blister. The method of applying these and other external remedies will be considered later.

Further, you must remember that the disorder is one of the whole system, and therefore the local joint affection passes readily from one to another, for example, from the knee to the wrist, from the elbow to the ankle. And so it will be your duty to see that no arm or even hand becomes exposed (as might readily be done in order to read a newspaper or book) till the physician's permission is obtained. A sour smelling profuse perspiration is a characteristic symptom of the disease which often causes considerable discomfort. Should this be the case you may dry the skin with a warmed towel, but it must be done quickly, and with as little exposure as possible.

It is right that you should know also that the great complication of acute rheumatism is heart disease. You must at once then report any sudden rise in temperature, complaint of oppression over the heart, palpitation, or similar symptom, which often indicates the beginning of cardiac mischief.

There is one point connected with a special treatment that you should know. A recent and much approved remedy in rheumatism is salicylic acid or salicylate of soda, and it is often given until its effects on the system, apart from its influence on the disease, are observed. These are sickness, deafness or ringing in the ears, giddiness on sitting up in bed, and such like. In some cases it may be left to you to continue giving the medicine till one or other of these effects is noticed.

Lastly, you must always remember the great liability the disease has to relapse or to return. You will be careful therefore to carry out to the letter all directions as to the avoidance of draughts, exposure to cold, etc., even when the patient appears to have quite recovered.

I might here in a sentence or two refer to another disease in which a special dietary is sometimes part of the treatment, viz.:—

ANEURISM.—If a particular part of an artery, owing to some kind of disease of its walls, yields under the pressure of the blood and becomes dilated, an aneurism is said to have formed. If the affected artery comes within the possibility of operative interference it falls to the care of the surgeon: it is usually aortic aneurism,* either thoracic or abdominal with which the physician has to deal. The great object of treatment is to further the formation of clots within what is called the *sac* of the aneurism, and with this view perfect rest and a restricted diet are frequently enforced. You may be directed to keep the patient absolutely in the recumbent position, perhaps for many weeks, and to give at the same time a limited and always carefully measured amount of milk, and a certain weight of bread and meat, the exact quantities being laid down for you.

DIABETES.—We come now to a disease in which an exact diet is one of the essentials of treatment, while it leads us to a new class of disorders in which the kidneys are directly or indirectly affected. Diabetes is characterised mainly by the passage of a large amount of urine, accompanied by constant thirst. The

* The aorta is the main artery of the body. It rises from the heart, arches over the root of the left lung to the back of the chest, and then passes down in front of the spinal column into the abdominal cavity, where it divides into two branches.

former symptom early attracted attention, and for a long time it was thought to be an affection of the kidneys. But it is now known to be an obscure disorder of some of the processes of nutrition. The food that is taken into the system is somehow not dealt with as it ought to be; the result being that a large amount of sugar is continually present in the blood. It is in the endeavour to carry off this unnatural constituent of the blood that the kidneys act so energetically; and we find the urine contains a large quantity of sugar.

You must understand so much of the nature of this disease in order to carry out intelligibly the dietetic treatment which will likely be left entirely to your care. It is usual to give no food which contains sugar or which can be readily converted into sugar; in other words, we select a diet *free from both the saccharine and the starchy principles of food.* Now, while the physician will indicate with more or less detail the diet suitable for the particular case, it is well that you should have for reference a list of such articles of food as are admissible in diabetes and also those specially inadmissible.

Note, then, that all kinds of animal food may be given—butcher meat, poultry, game, fish, eggs, cream, butter, and cheese. Soups are allowable if not made with any of the vegetables forbidden below. They must not be thickened with flour, rice, vermicelli, etc. The vegetables that may be taken are cabbage, greens, spinach, Brussels-sprouts, lettuce, water cresses, and green vegetables generally. All kinds of sour fruits; strawberries, too, appear to be quite suitable. Tea, coffee, and cocoa generally agree well, but they must not of course, be sweetened with sugar; glycerine has been found to be a fairly good substitute for the latter.

On the other hand, the following must be strictly forbidden—potatoes, turnips, parsnips, peas, beans, etc.; rice, barley, arrowroot, sago, etc.; anything made from ordinary oatmeal or wheaten flour, for example, pastry of all kinds; sweet puddings also must be forbidden, and still more all confectionery.

Mistakes are often made inadvertently. The addition of sugar itself to tea is not an uncommon one. But the great difficulty that demands our attention is the craving for the forbidden food. That is almost certain to occur sooner or later, despite all the little artifices of the most accomplished cook. The craving calls for a new duty on your part, one something like that of, shall I say, a watchman. I have known a worthy patient in hospital so tempted as to steal his neighbour's dinner. It may be considered advisable to yield a little to this obvious craving of the system, but this is a question solely for the physician. Bread or biscuit is perhaps as much missed as anything. If the starchy principles of wheat be excluded, and only the gluten taken, so as to get what is called gluten flour, then bread, biscuits, and all kinds of pastry made from it are quite admissible. Diabetic biscuits are prepared by many bakers and are also sold by druggists. Van Abbott of London prepares a great variety of diabetic foods, which may also be obtained through a druggist.

You will often be directed to measure the quantity of fluid swallowed and also the amount of urine passed in the 24 hours. This amount normally is about 50 ounces. In diabetes it may reach 5, 10, or even 20 pints. You should be able to recognise what is called *Fehling's solution*, one of the tests for saccharine urine, and know that it should be kept in a stoppered bottle and in a cool and dark place. We shall refer to this, however, again when we come to the examination of urine, which must be deferred till next lecture.

I shall conclude with a general reference to :—

DISEASES OF THE KIDNEY.—You will understand how serious is any continued impairment of their function when you reflect what that function is. It is to carry off certain waste material from the system, material which is both useless and an offence to the system—a positive poison if not got rid of. This waste is held in solution by the urine, and is thus carried off, along with a certain amount of super-abundant fluid. The waste of substances which contain carbon and hydrogen—mainly the fatty and saccharine principles—is discharged by the lungs as carbonic acid, but the nitrogenous compounds—those of the first four divisions of the food I mentioned, the albuminous or fibrinous—produce in addition a waste product called *urea*, which is carried off by the kidneys. Uraemic poisoning is the name given to a certain comatose condition, supposed to depend on a poisoned state of the blood connected with the non-excretion of this urea.

Several diseases of the kidney having a certain connection with each other are included under the term *Bright's Disease*—a term you will often hear. Dr. Bright, an English physician, was the first who associated albumen in the urine and dropsy with disease of the kidney. Albumen is a natural constituent of the blood, but not of the urine, and its presence in the latter is the result generally of some morbid change in the blood or in the structure of the kidney. Dropsy is the effusion of watery fluid from the blood into the tissues immediately under the skin or into certain cavities of the body. It may or may not depend upon disease of the kidney; it is often the result of disease of the heart.

Special forms of dropsy have special names which you will often hear employed. *Ascites* is dropsy of the abdominal cavity. *Œdema* is dropsy in the tissues of some particular part. When a considerable portion of the body is dropsical, it is called *anasarca*. We speak of general anasarca, but we say œdema of the foot, or of the eyelid, etc. If, say, a foot is œdematous, it is swollen, the skin is tense, white, and glazed-looking, and on pressing upon it with the finger-tips, their imprint will remain for a time. The part is then said to "pit on pressure." Debility alone may cause œdema of the foot or leg.

QUESTIONS ON LECTURE V.

1. What is the dietetic treatment of
   a. Diarrhœa?
   b. Scurvy?

2. Describe the cause, nature, and symptoms of rickets.

3. What is the general treatment of scrofula?

4. What are the special precautions necessary in nursing a case of acute rheumatism?

5. In a case of diabetes, what kind of food is inadmissible? and give a few examples of such food.

6. What is the function of the kidney?

7. What is meant by the terms "Bright's Disease," Ascites, Œdema, Anasarca, and "Pitting on pressure"?

LECTURE VI.

THE EXAMINATION OF THE URINE—CHARACTER OF THE MOTIONS FROM THE BOWELS—THE NERVOUS SYSTEM AND ITS DISEASES—APOPLEXY—EPILEPSY—FAINTING —PARALYSIS.

THE EXAMINATION OF THE URINE.—This in hospital is an every-day occurrence, and is performed according to a systematic method. It is seldom omitted, and always carried out with care; the results obtained being often a valuable guide, not only to the diagnosis of the different forms of renal disease, but to many general disorders of the system. It will only be in very exceptional circumstances that any part of that examination will devolve upon you.

On the other hand, the apparatus required will constantly be under your charge; and you will probably be expected to know something of the special tests and the particular apparatus necessary for the commoner investigations. I propose, therefore, to show you and explain to you one or two methods of examining or testing urine, and the reagents we employ for that purpose.

But first as to the time when specimens should be taken. The urine is far from having a constant composition even in health. It always contains more solid matter while digestion is going on; and on the other hand, is diluted if a considerable quantity of water has shortly before been drunk. It is usually collected, therefore, for examination in the morning, before it is influenced by either of the above circumstances. Glasses of a special shape are used for containing the specimens, which admit of some general characters of the urine being more perfectly appreciated by the eye, and they are besides cleanly and convenient where many specimens are collected.

The number of these, even in connection with one set of wards, is always considerable; and accordingly certain precautions are required in order that each specimen may be identified. I shall put these in the form of a rule which in hospital should be strictly adhered to. It is this. A slip of paper is to be attached to each specimen, and on this must be written *the number of the ward, the patient's name, the number of his bed, and the date of collection.* If this is always done, there will be no mistake made, even though there should chance to be two patients of the same name in one ward, or though the same specimen should be kept for comparison over several days.

We note first the general appearance of the urine, for example, the depth of colour, the degree of transparency, etc. The amount of colour usually depends simply on the extent to which the urine is diluted. It ought to be clear when passed. The milky cloudiness, often very dense, which only appears as the urine cools, is usually as unimportant as it is popularly alarming. But if it is turbid when passed, it must be kept for examination. There is also a peculiar smoky tint that indicates the presence of blood, which it would be well if you could recognise.

CHEMICAL EXAMINATION OF THE URINE.—
Of all such examinations, that for *albumen* in
the urine is the most common. You will
remember I told you that its presence there is
quite unnatural, and is one of the symptoms
of Bright's Disease. For the examination of
albuminous urine, you will have ready, in
addition to the specimen itself, the following
apparatus: one or two test tubes, a spirit
lamp, and nitric acid. You will observe the
examiner put some of the urine into a test
tube and heat it to the boiling point over the
spirit lamp. If the urine loses its clearness,
and a milky cloudiness appears, there is probably albumen; there is certainly albumen
present if the addition of a little nitric acid
does not make the urine clear again.

Before making this examination, the examiner may, and in all delicate enquiries will,
wish to test the *reaction* of the urine, that is
to say, will wish to know if it is acid or alkaline. For that purpose you will provide him
with test paper. It is usually supplied in
little boxes, containing both blue and red
litmus paper. Acid urine will make the blue

litmus paper red, and alkaline urine will make the red litmus paper blue.

Again a special instrument called a *urinometer* is required, that we may take the *specific gravity* of the urine. Gravity means weight, and the specific gravity of a body is its weight compared with that of a specific or special thing, namely pure water; it being always taken as the standard with which everything else is compared.

Urine is somewhat heavier or denser than water. The specific gravity of the latter being called 1, or for convenience 1000, that of normal urine is from 1015 to 1020. Now, just as a thermometer is made according to a fixed standard for taking the temperature, so a urinometer is made with numbers on its stem for taking the specific gravity. If the urine becomes denser or of greater consistence, as we might say, so much the less will the urinometer sink in it, and a correspondingly higher number on its stem will coincide with the level of the water; for the instrument is so graduated that the number on the stem at that level indicates the specific gravity. The specific gravity of diabetic urine may be as high as 1045.

The great test of diabetic urine is Fehling's solution. It consists of 1 part of a copper solution to 4 parts of an alkaline solution. These two solutions are frequently kept in separate bottles till the urine comes to be tested, as the mixture is apt to undergo changes which render it unreliable. Before using, they are mixed, then boiled, and the suspected urine added very gradually. If sugar is present the blue colour will be changed to a yellowish brown. Liquor potassae may also be wanted as a test in suspected diabetes, and in other cases as well. You should at least know these names.

Besides the substances held in solution by the urine, you will often find some that have fallen as a deposit to the bottom of the urine glass. These sediments, or urinary deposits as they are called, come under examination also. For that we require a pipette and a microscope with glass slides, etc. I need not describe them. You will see that the urine glasses, pipette, glass slides, and all the apparatus indeed, are kept thoroughly clean; and that the microscope is protected from the dust with at least a towel, and kept out of the way of meddlesome fingers.

CHARACTER OF THE STOOLS.—You will be expected to note their frequency in the 24 hours, whether in relation to a special disease or to some purgative administered. You will note if they are loose or watery; if there is anything peculiar in their colour; or if the food is evidently not wholly digested (lienteric motions).

The motions typical of enteric fever (of which disease we shall speak at next lecture), are liquid, and have a yellow ochre colour. In jaundice they are conspicuously light in colour from deficiency of bile. Intestinal hæmorrhage, unless the bleeding be from the lower end of the bowel, will darken or even blacken the stools. But so also will all remedies containing iron or bismuth. You must be careful not to be misled by this circumstance. If the hæmorrhage is from the last part of the bowel, the blood will be unchanged in appearance. Foreign bodies such as worms

THE NERVOUS SYSTEM. 107

should never be overlooked. All the peculiarities I have mentioned, unless they are caused by the above-mentioned drugs, require that the motions be kept for further inspection.

We have now concluded another distinct division of our course. Diseases of the various organs have been considered, with diet as a more or less appropriate connecting link; and in passing I have referred to the functions of the respiratory, digestive, and urinary organs. The circulatory system comes more appropriately within the scope of your surgical course, so that we shall say nothing of it here, but pass to the consideration, very shortly, of :—

THE NERVOUS SYSTEM AND ITS DISEASES.— To go back to our old figure of a contest, we may consider the nervous system as holding much the same position in the animal economy as a commander-in-chief and his staff do towards the army in the field. The capability of action is there, in each brigade, regiment, company, down to each individual soldier; but as a fighting body every movement must emanate from one source—the general in command. And so, though every limb be perfect, every muscle and tendon there, yet all the movements of our body as a whole, must emanate from one source—the brain.

The brain is the seat of the mind: through it we feel and think and will; and having willed we send down through the nerves that rise from the brain, all our orders, as a general does by means of his staff.

But if we stopped here you would have a very imperfect, a very one-sided view, of the functions of the nervous system. It can do much more than carry orders from the brain to the various muscles; but we shall retain the simile we employed just a minute ago, to show how it will *not* illustrate all that can be done by the nervous system. The individual soldier does not send his impressions up through captain, colonel, and the higher commanding officers for the information and guidance of the commander-in-chief. But every point, every unit, so to speak, of our body, sends impressions by a particular class of nerves to the brain. Should these impressions set us

THE BRAIN AND THE MIND. 109

thinking, we may or may not then exercise our will to do something, according as we judge this to be necessary or not. With the point of my finger I touch this table, and at once (*apparently* at once, for it really does take some little time) the impression of the table being there, of its smoothness, etc., is conveyed to my brain and to my mind. Had I felt it to be wet I would have lifted this sheet of paper out of the way. The impression having been conveyed to my mind, I would have judged the paper to be in danger and would have willed to remove it. Another set of nerves, those first referred to, would then have carried the order to particular muscles by which I would have placed my hand on the paper, grasped it and lifted it away. All this is effected through what is called the *cerebro-spinal* system of nerves; consisting as it does of the brain or *cerebrum*, the spinal cord, and the nerves arising therefrom.

But besides these actions of ours depending on impressions made and will exercised, you know there are many processes going on within our bodies, independent of our thoughts and beyond our control. Our heart beats and our stomach digests food as if by a will of their own; and, as we have already seen, thinking about our respiration, over which we have some control, only interferes with its natural rhythm. These functions and those of the other internal organs are carried on in great part by another system of nerves called the *sympathetic system*. The two systems are intimately connected, but they may be practically viewed as distinct. What is within our control is done through the cerebro-spinal system; what is beyond it, is carried on by the sympathetic. As Dr. Hinton says, " the constant processes of life are withdrawn from our concern. . . . Thus the nobler part of us is set free to attend to worthy objects, and the truly human life is erected, as on a pedestal, upon the animal life which serves it, and which should ever be held as its servant."

It is unnecessary for me to attempt here anything like an anatomical description of the nervous system. There are able elementary works on physiology where this is all

THE NERVOUS SYSTEM. 111

well told. It will be sufficient to give you merely an outline sketch of the subject.

The brain, which is the great centre of the nervous system, is enclosed by the skull, and is the seat of consciousness and the source of all voluntary movement. From it spring directly the nerves of smell, sight, hearing, etc., and many others. It is continued in the spinal cord which runs down the back, within the bony canal formed by the spine. From the spinal cord rise the nerves which go to the skin and to the muscles of the body. Part of their fibres are known to be sensory and form the nerves of sensation. They convey impressions *to* the brain and are therefore called afferent* nerves. The other part of their fibres are motor, and form the nerves which convey *from* the brain the order and ability to the muscles to move. They are therefore called efferent† nerves.

The spinal cord, besides being the medium for the transmission of impulses to and from the brain, has a power of its own, which

---

* Latin, *ad*, to, and *fero*, I carry.
† Latin, *e*, from, and *fero*, I carry.

becomes apparent if this connection with the brain is cut off in any way. Suppose this connection is cut off from disease or injury of the spinal cord, the result is paralysis of the lower limbs and of all parts below the seat of mischief. Now pinch one foot slightly. The patient feels nothing; in other words no impression is carried to the brain; but the paralysed, the helpless limbs, over which he has no control, in all probability give a sudden jerk, or perhaps move repeatedly. The impulse given by the pinch cannot be conveyed to the brain; but now the spinal cord has the power of reflecting it as it were, and it is sent down again by the motor nerves of the limb to various muscles which are thereby called into action. This is termed *reflex action*.

I cannot make this of much practical value to you as regards nervous diseases, of which indeed I intend to say very little, but what I have told you will perhaps help you to understand many curious phenomena connected with disorders of this kind.

What I have to say about nervous affections will be confined almost entirely to two kinds of emergency cases that one may meet with anywhere; and something of the treatment of which concerns not us alone, but every one. I refer to the diseases:—

APOPLEXY AND EPILEPSY.—Their names are similar, their symptoms are not unlike, but in their nature they are very different. They are both diseases that come on suddenly as an attack or fit; the patient becomes unconscious and will fall if unsupported. One may meet with them at any time. They both require immediate attention; while they both by their symptoms impress the inexperienced onlooker with the conviction that he is unable to render it. You must therefore be familiar with them, that they may not terrify you from doing the little that it is right to do; and you must know what that is. Just a word or two then, about their nature and symptoms as well as their treatment.

Apoplexy is the result of some form of structural weakness of the brain, and is always attended by considerable danger and the risk of permanent disability. It is a disease of later life. The loss of consciousness is usually sudden, but may be gradual. Convulsive movements are not so constant as with epilepsy; the breathing is likely to be deep, heavy, or stertorous.

Epilepsy, on the other hand, is a purely functional disorder; that is to say, it depends upon no definite structural disease of the brain. It is not dangerous; the patient will likely have had previous attacks and may be quite young. The loss of consciousness is sudden, and if he is standing he will at once fall. At first there is rigid spasm of the muscles, but in a few seconds both face and limbs become strongly convulsed and he probably froths at the mouth. After one or a few minutes this ceases, he regains consciousness but soon falls into a sleep, from which he awakens remembering nothing of what has occurred. Such are the more characteristic symptoms of each disease, but you must understand that on coming across a case of either, perhaps as you pass along the street, you may find it impossible to say at once which of the two it is.

Let us consider now what everyone should

APOPLEXY AND EPILEPSY. 115

know something about;—the "first aid" to the sufferer. In both affections the patient should have plenty of air. Open the windows therefore, or make the crowd stand back, according to circumstances. Loosen everything about the neck, and protect the tongue, if it is liable to be bitten from convulsive movements of the jaw, by placing a pencil, cork, or such like, between the teeth. Do not restrain the convulsive movements except so far as to prevent the patient hurting himself. When we add that in epilepsy the patient should lie on his back with the head low, we have mentioned all that you need do in that affection. In apoplexy there is one important difference in the treatment—*the head and shoulders must be raised.* Till medical assistance is obtained you may apply cold water or iced water cloths to the head, and mustard poultices to the calves of the legs.

FAINTING OR SYNCOPE may simply be noticed here in passing. It arises from weakness of the system generally, or from some sudden shock, or loss of blood sufficient to affect the heart's action. It is the direct result of a diminution in the force of the circulation, by which particularly the supply of blood to the brain is for the time much lessened. It is easily distinguished from apoplexy or epilepsy by pallor of the countenance throughout the attack, flaccidity of the muscles, and the absence of convulsions.

The patient should be laid on the back with the head brought to the same level as the body. The dress, if tight, should be loosened, especially about the neck; and the face bathed with cold water. As much fresh air as possible should be admitted. If caused by the loss of blood, that will probably have already attracted attention; meanwhile, till medical assistance is obtained, it will be better to withhold any form of stimulant. The fainting, or rather the accompanying diminution in the force of the circulation, will, for the time, lessen the risk of further hæmorrhage, a risk that stimulants might increase.

I shall, in concluding this part of our subject, do little more than mention some forms of paralysis that come under our observation. Apoplexy is often followed by paralysis: a "shock" or "stroke," as it is called. Such forms of paralysis usually attack one side of the body only, although the face and the body may be affected on different sides. We always note with interest the indications of returning power: they are generally observed in the leg earlier than in the arm. This one-sided form of paralysis is termed *hemiplegia*.

Then there is paralysis of the lower half of the body, which we call *paraplegia*. It is usually the result of injury or disease of the spinal cord, and is the form of paralysis in which we see those involuntary reflex movements to which I referred a short time ago. The patient lies powerless in bed, so far at least as the lower half of his body is concerned; and yet he may be continually tormented by movements which he is equally unable to set agoing or control.

But I need not say more on this subject. The one thing which it is your special duty to remember in such affections is the great liability to the formation of bedsores. In a well-marked case of paralysis there are three reasons for this:—

1st. The patient lies helpless in one position.

2nd. He may not be sensible of any discomfort, such as would lead him to ask to be moved into a different position; and

3rd. The vitality of the skin itself is impaired.

The all-important question of the treatment of bedsores will be considered later on.

QUESTIONS ON LECTURE VI.

1. What precautions are required in order that the different specimens of urine may be identified?

2. Mention the commoner apparatus which you should have ready for the examination of urine.

3. Explain the principles on which a urinometer is constructed.

4. What peculiarities in the motions should be noted by you?

5. Explain the function of an afferent and of an efferent nerve?

6. In what respects do apoplexy and epilepsy resemble each other, and in what do they differ?

7. What is meant by the terms "Hemiplegia," "Paraplegia," and "Reflex action"?

LECTURE VII.

The Infectious Fevers — Typhus Fever — Enteric Fever — Scarlet Fever — Measles — Hooping Cough — Diphtheria.

To-day we begin the consideration of a new class of diseases—the Infectious Fevers. I do not intend to take up in detail all that relates to fever nursing. We have no cases of fever in this hospital, and in itself the subject is too wide, as well as too special, for a general course like this. What I shall aim at will be to mention such points as will help you to recognise a case of fever should it unexpectedly cross your path; and give you, at the same time, the general line of treatment you will be directed to carry out, and the precautions you should take to prevent the spread of infection.

When we speak of a case of fever we most

probably refer to one of three—typhus, enteric (typhoid), or scarlet fever. But there are many other diseases which are true infectious fevers; for example, measles, hooping cough, diphtheria, etc., not to mention small-pox, which is now, fortunately, little seen in general practice. I shall not say anything of it, but make a few remarks on the others I have just mentioned; and first:—

TYPHUS FEVER.—A spotted fever, running a high course though a comparatively short one; all the more dangerous while it lasts, and requiring the closest attention and the most skilled nursing: such is typhus fever.

The infection is conveyed through the atmosphere, and is rendered more powerful or active by the neglect of the ordinary laws of health; such as want of cleanliness, overcrowding and imperfect ventilation. On the other hand, attention to such laws readily prevents it spreading. I shall give you the simplest outline of its course, and in such a way that you may contrast it with the fever to be considered immediately afterwards.

Typhus fever is sudden in its onset; be-

TYPHUS FEVER.

ginning sometimes with well-marked shivering, though oftener preceded for a day or two by a wearied aching feeling in the back and limbs. Headache sets in early, the patient quickly feels exhausted, and takes readily to bed. The eyes are bloodshot, and the face inclines to a dark flush. The bowels are probably confined.

About the fifth or sixth day a rash appears, consisting of small round dusky spots, with no very defined outline; partly because the colour of the spots runs, as it were, or shades off, and partly because the background, the skin generally, is tinged a dusky hue; the whole forming an ill-defined mottled or marbled appearance. The rash is seen most usually on the abdomen, chest, back, and limbs; and on the third day after its appearance the spots are all out. They will cease then to disappear under the pressure of the finger.

About this time (the end of the first week) the headache usually ceases, but delirium and weakness increase; the patient requiring closer and closer attention till about the fourteenth day when the crisis or "turn" is reached.

With this the danger is past, and sudden and rapid improvement takes place. I mention these symptoms more by way of contrast, as I have said, to those of enteric fever, which we shall consider immediately, somewhat more at length.

The nursing of typhus is one of constant care. Everything must be done that can relieve the symptoms and support the strength. In no other fever is the patient's helplessness likely to be so marked. The body is prostrate, and the mind runs riot. Then "the nurse," as my friend Dr. Allan says, "must *think* and *act* for the patient. All the wants of nature, all the requirements of decency, will be neglected unless she interposes." I have quoted from an authority whose *Notes on Fever Nursing* will be invaluable to any of you who intend to take up this duty specially; and to that work I refer you for full details of the nursing of typhus.

ENTERIC FEVER.—This is sometimes called "typhoid fever," but that term has the objection, amongst others, of making one imagine it is a modification of typhus, and so it is popularly supposed to be, and a modification for the worse; whereas it is quite a distinct fever. A mild attack is often called "gastric fever." It has little resemblance to typhus. It is longer continued, not so conspicuously dangerous at any one time, but uncertain in its course, and often deceptive in its indications of recovery; the crisis is not so marked, and with it the danger is not altogether past.

The disease is not conveyed from the patient directly, but through the discharges from the bowels. Practically, it is found that contaminated drinking-water is the most common medium of infection, and, more recently, milk so poisoned has been proved to be a fruitful source of it. But this arises from accidental circumstances; chiefly bad drainage; for anything contaminated by enteric excreta may become a cause. It is not dependent on immediate insanitary surroundings, and therefore may attack the rich as readily as the poor.

Enteric fever concerns you as general medical nurses much more than typhus; for you may meet with it, and have to attend it, now and then in any hospital. Being commoner, too, amongst the better classes, you may have a case of it in private, as the patient is often kept at home, and may be nursed there in comparative safety.

It invades the system gradually, and for several days the patient may complain of little else than "heats and colds," some headache, and probably pains in the back and limbs. The *continuance* of these symptoms attracts attention, and spots will be searched for although there are no other characteristic symptoms. If, in addition, there is pain or pressure in the abdomen, and loose yellowish motions, the suspicion of enteric fever will be very strong.

The rash appears at a variable time; usually between the seventh and the twelfth day. It consists of round rose-coloured spots, which are pretty well defined as the skin is quite unaltered. They do not all appear at once, but come out in successive crops; each of about three days' duration. This is sometimes shown by surrounding the spots that appear, say to-day, with a little circle of ink; those of to-morrow to be surrounded by a square, and so on; and then watching when those of a particular day begin to fade. They are slightly raised and disappear under the pressure of the finger, and are usually seen, probably in no very great numbers, over the chest and abdomen.

Meanwhile, the abdominal pain and, as a rule, the diarrhœa continue. This will remind you that the bowels are the weak point in this fever; a fact which you must ever keep before you as the explanation and reason of a very definite treatment which you will be directed to carry out. Delirium though not so constant, nor as a rule so severe, as in typhus, may begin by the end of the second week, and will require your closest attention. Along with continual watchfulness it demands, to a striking degree, the exercise of these two apparently opposite qualities, gentleness and firmness; but firmness only when gentleness fails.

The crisis is not at all so decided as in typhus; and when convalescence has apparently begun a relapse may occur with a repetition of all the old symptoms.

The treatment will be mainly directed to the condition of the bowels. Of course, the patient will be kept strictly in bed. "It is a good rule," says Murchison, "never to allow the patient to get out of bed to the night-stool, after the tenth day of his illness, until convalescence is fairly established." At the same time it is of great service, as in typhus fever, to have two beds in the room, so that the patient may be changed from the one to the other, perhaps twice in the 24 hours. "The change," says Murchison again, "will sometimes procure sleep after other measures have failed."

Milk, given in small quantities at a time, will likely be the diet prescribed. Your great duty is to see that *nothing else is given*, either by yourself or another, without orders. Probably you will be directed to give, in addition, a little ice, soda water, or lime water.

A characteristic feature in the treatment of enteric fever is the necessity for continued care even when convalescence has apparently begun. And especially with regard to diet is this necessary. The patient begins now to feel really hungry, and craves for a change. But with the physician must rest all the responsibility in this respect; such as allowing beef-tea, chicken soup, arrowroot, etc. With every care a relapse may occur, but you must be careful to give no occasion for it.

As to stimulants you have only to give the exact amount you are told to give, and at the exact time stated.

The treatment of special symptoms will be indicated by the doctor. It may include the application of poultices, fomentations, etc., which we shall consider by and by.

Involuntary evacuations or, on the other hand, retention of urine should always be reported; the former requires careful attention, use of the draw-sheet, etc., to keep the patient clean, and prevent bed-sores forming. Sometimes dangerous bleeding occurs from the bowels. If so, give the patient some ice to suck, and apply iced cloths to the abdomen; and send for medical assistance.

Sudden acute abdominal pain and vomiting should be reported at once; probably perforation of the bowel will have occurred.

PREVENTION OF TYPHUS AND ENTERIC FEVERS.—To prevent typhus spreading, the first essential is free ventilation. All the windows in the house should, so far as possible, be kept open for the sake of the other inmates; and the more open spaces there are in the vicinity, the better for the neighbours. There is no risk of any one catching the disease who does not actually enter the sick-room. With the class amongst which typhus is most likely to break out, it is always best to remove the patient to the fever hospital *in the fever van.* Infected clothing, etc., should be treated as we shall see immediately under enteric fever and scarlet fever.

Enteric fever, you will remember, is conveyed through the excreta. It is not believed to be directly communicable from the patient. To prevent it spreading, attend to the following rules:—

1. Discharges to be received into vessels, and powdered freely over with cupralum,* or chloride of lime; the vessels to be washed afterwards with a solution of one or other of the foregoing, and some of this solution kept in them until they are required again.

* A pleasant smelling powder which can be obtained in small tins from any druggist.

PREVENTION OF ENTERIC FEVER.

2. A similar disinfectant solution to be poured down sinks, water-closets, etc., occasionally.

3. Bed and body linen to be put into an aqueous solution (1-40) of carbolic acid: *i.e.*, a wine-glassful of fluid carbolic acid to every gallon of water. (See also under prevention of scarlet fever.)

4. Drinking-water, milk, etc., to be boiled before being used.

I wish now to say a few words to you on scarlet fever and measles, that you may recognise them also, should they unexpectedly confront you, as well as have a general idea of their treatment.

SCARLET FEVER.—It is very often called Scarlatina, and this latter term does not signify a milder allied affection, as is sometimes popularly supposed. Scarlet fever is not intrinsically so infectious as measles; but owing to one circumstance—the shedding of the scarf skin in little dusty flakes, or in larger pieces during convalescence (*desquamation*, as it is called), which carry with them the infecting particles—that infection may remain about the house or on one's clothes in undiminished power for a long time, and be transmitted also to almost any distance.

The fever sets in suddenly: there is no time for a day or two's preliminary peevishness as in measles. The rash appears earlier than in any other fever. It may be seen on the very day that the child is first noticed to be ailing; most likely about the side of the neck, the inner surface of the arms, and the upper part of the chest. It begins as a collection of little red dots or points, which soon run together and cause a general red blush of the skin. The back of the mouth and throat is early red, and painful in most cases: somewhat later the small red *papillae* (the little elevated points which are dotted over the tongue naturally) project through the white coating on the tongue; forming what is called "the strawberry tongue."

I have said enough to guide you in recognising the disease; though indeed it presents itself in the most diverse forms. No other fever exhibits such varying degrees of severity in different cases, not only during the same epidemic in one locality, but in different members of the same family. In this connection two things must always be remembered. (1) That from the mildest case one may take the severest form of the disease; and (2) The mildest case demands equal care both throughout the fever and during convalescence. And these are just the questions that concern a nurse most directly in the case of scarlet fever; but in the reverse order.

1. How the patient should be cared for, particularly during convalescence. You must never overlook this, that however mild the case, there is always a liability to dropsy occurring during the later stages of the affection. The kidneys then somehow are apt to become affected and their functions disturbed. If so, a little swelling or œdema under the eyes will likely be observed, and albumen found in the urine. To prevent this if possible taking place, the patient should be carefully protected from cold or draughts. While in bed he should be always well covered with the blankets, and when allowed to get up should wear flannels, and remain in the warm room and clear of all draughts till express

permission to leave his bedroom is given by the doctor.

2. How is infection to be prevented? Besides the ordinary precautions the most particular care must be taken to prevent the little flakes of skin already referred to from escaping with their dangerous freight. For each is laden with infecting particles as potent for mischief, under favourable circumstances, as any war *materiel* ever invented.

As soon as there is the least appearance of desquamation the body should be rubbed over daily with some kind of oil: camphorated oil does very well. This prevents the flakes from flying about the room, and admits of them being wiped off with a rag and burned; or after a time washed off with a bath, tepid at first, and carbolic soap. All dust in the room should be carefully collected and burned, and the simple expedient of shaking the patient's stockings over the fire after they have been worn for the day, will often lead to a wholesale destruction of dangerous germs. As regards the sick-room itself, everything that would harbour dust, everything that cannot be readily washed, everything indeed *not needed*, should be removed.

Desquamation will in all probability continue long after the patient is able to be out of bed and dressed. In that case his wearing apparel as well as bedclothes will require to be disinfected. To this I shall refer immediately. All the members of the family who have not had scarlet fever will probably have been sent from home; meantime, besides the precautions required as regards the sick-room, the whole house should be kept thoroughly ventilated, as I mentioned should be done in the case of typhus fever.

I shall now give you in tabular form for convenient reference, some generally recognised rules for the prevention of scarlet fever.

1. Separate the patient completely from the other inmates, and to the top of the house if this can be done.
2. Hang a sheet, kept wet with a 1-40 aqueous solution of carbolic acid, outside the door of the patient's bedroom. (I only mention this rule as one that you may be sometimes told to observe.)
3. Cups, glasses, spoons, &c., and one's own hands, to be washed in carbolic acid solution (1-40) after having been in contact with the patient.

4. Bed and body linen to be put into carbolic acid solution (1-40) for half-an-hour, or into boiling water before being removed from the room, to be washed afterwards in the ordinary way, and exposed for a time to the fresh air. (Should there be of necessity any delay in carrying out the above, rather put them into a tub of simple water, which you will have in the sick-room, than have them lying dry in a corner of the room.)

5. The nurse in all cases to wear a cotton print or some dress that is easily washed.

6. The inunction of camphorated oil during desquamation, or warm baths with carbolic acid soap as already mentioned.

As to the disinfection of bedding, that had better be done by the sanitary authorities. But it may be ripped up, and the "ticks" treated as the other bed linen. Hair may be put in boiling water and feathers exposed to steam.

In no other fever is it so necessary to have the bedroom disinfected, so I shall describe here how that is conveniently done. You must see that the room has only such furniture remaining in it as will not be damaged by sulphur fumes. Put some pieces of sulphur or brimstone (one pound or so) on a shovel or iron lid, and set this on a brick which has been placed in a pail containing water to the depth of an inch or two. Then carefully close the windows, fireplace, and all crevices; and having done so set fire to the sulphur with one or two pieces of live coal, and make your way out of the room immediately, and shut the door. With the precautions mentioned there can be no danger of setting anything on fire except the sulphur. Let the room be fumigated for six hours; and then open windows and doors to admit of free ventilation. Afterwards the paper should be stripped from the wall, the room repapered, and the ceiling white-washed.

MEASLES.—The few words I have to say of this common affection are chiefly to contrast it with scarlet fever. Measles is a very infectious disease; few children escape it. For three or four days before the rash appears, the child is probably fretful; it is at least obviously ailing. There is catarrh of the nasal passages, or the congestion may be chiefly about the eyes, causing them to be intolerant of light.

The rash appears on the fourth day or even later, and is first seen on the face, most likely about the forehead or the temples. It usually appears as little round spots which run together into patches.

The characteristic symptom of measles is catarrh, and the great object of treatment is to prevent it passing down into the chest and becoming a complication. The patient must be kept strictly in bed, well covered by the clothes, and in a comfortably-warmed room, till the doctor indicates that this is no longer necessary.

HOOPING COUGH is really an infectious fever, but it does not require any very special nursing. It is infectious through the atmosphere, and apparently to a considerable distance. The infection seems to be capable of being carried by the clothing also; but I need not say that the mere hearing the cough will never cause infection, as is popularly supposed.

The number of coughs is sometimes directed

to be counted. It is usually greater and the coughs more severe during the night, and a diminution in this respect, as I mentioned in a previous lecture, is considered by Dr. West to be one of the most frequent indications that the disease has begun to lessen.

DIPHTHERIA, too, may be considered an infectious fever. It is a general blood-poisoning, of which the throat mischief is the localised expression. From the mucous membrane of the back of the mouth and throat an exudation takes place, which forms the pellicle or false membrane which characterises the disease.

In a severe case there is always great prostration, requiring the most nourishing diet, as beef-tea, cream, egg-flip, etc., given at regular intervals and in prescribed quantities. You will get precise directions also as to the kind and amount of stimulant, and how often it is to be given.

The disease being infectious chiefly through the discharges from the mouth and nose, you will be careful to clear away anything that is coughed up with a soft rag, which is to be immediately burned. You will probably be expected to keep the room at a higher temperature than in most other diseases, namely from 65° to 70° Fah. Should you be directed to have a moist atmosphere round the patient, you will require a kettle with a pipe, by means of which the steam from it may be carried near to the patient. A blanket tent for him also is sometimes ordered; it may be made with blankets hung round and over an ordinary clothes screen.

During convalescence you will on no account allow the patient even to sit up in bed without the express permission of the medical attendant. Fatal syncope might be induced by suddenly leaving the recumbent position.

QUESTIONS ON LECTURE VII.

1. How is infection conveyed in the case of :—
    a Typhus fever ?
    b Enteric fever ?
    c Scarlet fever ?

2. What was said regarding the dietetic treatment of enteric fever ?

3. Give the rules mentioned for preventing infection in enteric fever.

4. Detail the nursing of scarlet fever during convalescence.

5. How would you disinfect a sick-room after scarlet fever ?

6. What is the chief complication of measles, and what precautions should it lead to ?

LECTURE VIII.

The Prevention of Bedsores: External Applications—Fomentations—Poultices—A Fly Blister—Dry Heat—Cold Lotion—The Application of Ice—The Cold Compress.

In the past lectures I have brought under your notice those diseases, or those symptoms of disease, which I believe will best give you a fitting idea of the kind of cases you will, as medical nurses, have committed to your care. My object has been at the same time to direct your attention to such symptoms of disease as mark some of these important crises or complications, which it is essential should not escape the observation and care of the physician, but which may occur when you alone are there to see. We have now before us the last division of our course; the consideration of remedies, their administration, and in some instances their preparation.

But before entering upon this question, we may conveniently take up a most important subject, a complication in many diseases which is always in great part given over to your care and treatment; I refer to bedsores. I wish you, however, rather put down in your notebooks as the title of our subject:—

THE PREVENTION OF BEDSORES.—It is not so much their treatment as their prevention that you must always keep prominently before your mind.

A bedsore is the result of the death of a portion of skin, or it may be of the parts lying deeper, induced by the continued pressure of the bed on which the patient is lying. Undue pressure, if continuous, will at length destroy the vitality of any part of the body, even in a perfectly healthy person; but in weakened conditions of the system it is brought about much more readily. And the weaker the patient the more helpless does he lie in bed, so that the liability to bedsores increases twofold. Now it is the recognised duty of the nurse to prevent them forming if it is at all possible; and as to the possibility I thoroughly endorse the opinion generally held that *a good nurse will prevent the formation of a bedsore in nine cases out of ten in which a careless nurse will not.* This I believe to be no exaggeration, so that, if such be the case, you see your skill will frequently be put to the test in a very definite and unmistakable manner.

To come at once to the kind of malady in which bedsores are most liable to form, I would mention a case of pronounced paralysis. It is most likely to be the tenth case that will baffle all your skill and ingenuity. As I told you when we were speaking of paralysis, not only does the patient lie helpless in bed, not only is he less likely to feel pain from the pressure on the part, but the vitality of the skin itself is greatly lowered. In these circumstances, bedsores will readily form on any prominent part; the commonest situations being over the lower part of the back, and at the projections over each hip joint. There are undoubtedly some cases in which bedsores cannot be prevented, cases in which the ordinary pressure on the elbow or heel

THE PREVENTION OF BEDSORES. 143

determines their formation there; but these must be viewed as very exceptional.

As for your part in the matter, the first and universally accepted rule is—*Do not wait till the patient complains, but look for, nay, even anticipate the first indication of weakness of the skin.* And what is the first indication? It is usually one of these two. Either the patient complains of some itching or irritation about the part, perhaps imagining that the sheet is ruffled when it is really quite smooth, or else there is a little blush of redness on the skin over a prominence; this redness it is expected you will have discovered for yourself. If the sensibility of the skin be unimpaired, the patient may be the first to draw your attention to it, but he should not be, at least in any case where there is the least likelihood of such a thing occurring. Any illness accompanied by weakness or emaciation, particularly if the patient can lie only in one or two positions, or still more if there is any loss of control over the discharges, should at once suggest to your mind the liability to bedsores.

If the first symptoms are neglected, the part becomes swollen or puffy, the redness gradually assumes a darker or bluish hue, and a slough at length forms and separates, leaving an unsightly surface, and revealing probably a much greater loss of tissue than you were at all prepared for. Now as I have said, it is the prevention of all this that you must aim at, and the following are the principal points to which you must attend, besides being on the outlook for the first symptoms.

Keep the sheet on which the patient is lying smooth and tight and dry; if a drawsheet is used, tuck it firmly in at the sides of the bed to insure this. See that no bread crumbs, for example, or any similar cause of irritation, be allowed about the sheets, and change the patient's position in bed as often as other circumstances will allow.

Then with regard to the skin itself. Wash the parts carefully with soap and water at least night and morning, and be most particular in drying them thoroughly afterwards with a soft towel. This not merely insures cleanliness and the removal of the natural

TREATMENT OF BEDSORES.

exudation on the surface of the skin, which cannot in the circumstances readily escape, but positively strengthens and hardens the skin. This last effect is further increased by rubbing the skin with some form of spirit, *e.g.*, rectified spirit, which has the least smell, eau-de-Cologne, brandy, etc., or with an astringent lotion, such as a saturated solution of alum. The earlier such treatment is begun the better. In a case of paralysis it should always be begun before there is any appearance of redness. Should the redness appear to be spreading or deepening, or in any circumstances should the case likely be prolonged, a water-bed becomes essential.

If in spite of all precautions a bedsore forms, *stop all the above applications*, and treat it as you would an ordinary ulcer. If simple water-dressing or carbolised oil be applied, see that no part of the lint becomes uncovered by the gutta-percha tissue which you have placed over it, or it will soon become perfectly dry and adherent to the ulcer. It is not always easy to apply the dressing in such a way that this may not occur from the move-

K

ments of the patient. In these circumstances, you will find it a good plan to try an ounce of zinc ointment to which half an ounce of glycerine has been added, for this, if spread on lint, will keep moist for a considerable time without gutta-percha tissue over the lint.

In changing any of these dressings, the ulcer should be gently washed, and in the case of a zinc ointment application, a little simple or carbolised oil will be required occasionally to clear away some of the zinc powder, which is always apt to dry in.

We come now to the question of remedies. It is well that we should consider them separately, because they are usually administered or prepared by you, always, it must be understood, by the instructions of the medical attendant. We shall begin with:—

EXTERNAL REMEDIES, or remedies usually applied to the surface of the body. A nurse is certainly expected to be thoroughly conversant with all details relating to them, that they may be properly prepared and applied without a repetition of special instructions for each case. I know that you have had, or will have, practical demonstrations from the matron of what we are about to consider (the interest and value of which I have myself experienced), but still it is proper in a systematic course to consider the nature of such measures and the reasons for adopting them. We shall take first :—

FOMENTATIONS.—A fomentation is a local application of hot water by means of flannel, in such a form that *warmth* and *moisture* are combined and sustained. It is employed chiefly to lessen inflammation, allay pain, or relieve spasm. You require boiling water, flannel (preferably coarse flannel), and waterproof or macintosh. Oiled silk does not make a good substitute for the last. You prepare a fomentation in the following way:—

Spread out a towel in an empty basin, and on that lay the flannel folded eight times or so, and to the size you wish it. Then pour boiling water upon it, and wring it in the towel as dry as you possibly can. Keep it in the towel till you are ready to apply it to the patient, and just before doing so, shake it gently for a second or two to allow the admission of a little air between the folds of the flannel. Having applied it, place a piece of macintosh over it of such a size that the latter will completely overlap the flannel by at least an inch on all sides. See that the whole is kept closely in position by means of a bandage or such like. If you are careful to follow these instructions, a fomentation will continue hot for many hours; but if, for example, the macintosh should not completely overlap the flannel, should even a corner of the latter be exposed, evaporation will take place at that point, and the fomentation will become cold, clammy, and worse than useless. If properly applied, however, it will continue hot, as I have said, for many hours; but in most cases you will be directed to change it every hour or so.

Never omit to shake the fomentation in the way I mentioned, so as to separate the folds of the flannel somewhat. It is a point seldom referred to, and far too little known. The fomentation will not be materially cooled by so doing, while by being made less compact or solid, or, in other words, by having a freer admixture of air, which is a bad conductor of heat, the heat will be retained by the fomentation for a much longer time. Coarse flannel is preferable for the same reason; there is more air in its interstices.

On changing a fomentation, wipe the skin dry and immediately apply the next.

To relieve spasm, or act more as a counter-irritant, one or two teaspoonfuls of oil of turpentine are often added to the fomentation. It should be quickly sprinkled over the flannel just before the fomentation is applied. It is of great service in an attack of colic. To relieve pain more effectually a teaspoonful of laudanum may be added in the same way.

POULTICES are much the same as fomentations. They differ only in having some special ingredient as the medium in addition to the water, and in place of the flannel. They are also employed for much the same purposes. They are usually of linseed meal, but may be made with oatmeal, bread, starch, etc. A linseed and an oatmeal poultice retain heat and moisture longest.

Before making a poultice have everything heated that you are going to use—the basin, linen, spatula, etc. Begin by pouring boiling water into the basin sufficient for the size of the poultice, then quickly sprinkle in the linseed meal, stirring the while till the whole is of proper consistence. Spread it now on a piece of linen rather larger than the size of the poultice wanted, with a spatula which has been dipped in hot water, and turn the margins of linen left, over the sides of the poultice. Having applied it without anything between the poultice and the skin (for if properly made it will separate perfectly from the skin when taken off), place over it a piece of macintosh in the same way and for the same reason as in the case of a fomentation.

A bread poultice loses heat and moisture sooner than one of linseed, but it is a blander application. Prepare by cutting stale bread into small squares, and put them into a basin which has just been scalded. Pour boiling water over them, cover with a plate, and place by the fire for a few minutes. Then pour off the water, beat up lightly with a fork, and apply on a piece of linen. Sometimes a bread and milk poultice is ordered. Milk then is the medium in place of water, and the mode of preparation is the same.

A starch poultice is quite unirritating, and is often applied to inflamed skin eruptions. It is made simply as hot starch is prepared, and should be of such a consistence as to admit of it being spread on linen in the ordinary way.

All the foregoing, except the starch poultice, should be applied as hot as they can be borne.

A MUSTARD POULTICE.—This, as you all know, is quite a distinct form of poultice. It is always used as a counter-irritant, and is quicker in its action and causes more severe pain than a fly blister. Here I would just caution you not to fall into the error of speaking of a mustard *blister*. Mustard should never blister, and if it does so it is apt to leave a painful surface which is slow to heal.

A mustard poultice should be prepared with cold or tepid water; never with hot water, for that only sets free the active principles of the drug, and much of its strength is lost before the poultice is applied. The addition of vinegar also, only weakens the mustard. Having made it into a paste, spread it on a piece of linen, or on brown paper, to the size wished, and over the surface to be applied to the skin lay a piece of muslin. Fold over the margin of linen which has been left, as in the case of ordinary poultices.

A mustard poultice may be kept on fifteen, twenty, or twenty-five minutes: the time will vary according to the sensitiveness of the skin of the part. Some individuals are peculiarly sensitive to its action. On removing the poultice sponge the skin gently with tepid water, and apply a layer of cotton wool.

A mustard poultice is sometimes diluted with equal parts of linseed meal. When enough of the latter has been added to the boiling water the proportion of mustard should be put in. A common soothing application to the chest is a linseed meal poultice with about a teaspoonful of dry mustard sprinkled over its surface, the whole being covered with muslin and kept on for a longer or shorter period, according to the amount of redness desired.

A FLY BLISTER. 153

What is called mustard paper will be found a convenient substitute in some circumstances. Cut into different sizes, they are called mustard leaves, and may be obtained almost anywhere. A newer and better preparation is mustard plaster spread on cotton cloth. Small packets containing a few plasters of convenient size may be had at most druggists'. Whatever form is used, it should be moistened with a little tepid water before being applied.

A FLY BLISTER may either be in the form of a plaster or of a blistering fluid. It differs from a mustard plaster in being slower, less painful, but more penetrating in its action, and in being as a rule intended to blister. It is applied in cases of deeply seated or chronic inflammations, to relieve pain, as, for example, in neuralgia. The fluid is quicker in its action than the plaster.

The blister being prepared for you of the size ordered, you will probably find there is a small margin of adhesive plaster left. Do not make use of this to any great extent. If necessary it may be fixed more securely with a turn of a bandage. You may be directed to apply a small piece of tissue paper over the plaster, especially if the skin of the part be rather delicate.

A fly blister is usually kept on six or eight hours, but on thick-skinned parts, as the scalp, it may require ten or twelve hours, or more, to blister. As to the degree of blistering to be produced you will probably get explicit instructions. That will depend on many circumstances, such as the disease, the size of blister, the age, and state of the patient generally. But it is worth remembering as a general principle that the irritant effect is greater if the blisters break, or if we snip them with a pair of scissors, than if they are unbroken. We do not touch the vesicles or blebs produced by a burn, because the less irritation there is in that case the better, and the admission of air to the raw surface always irritates it; but we open the blebs of a fly blister if we wish a greater counter-irritant effect. If this is done, open the blister at the most dependent point, and do not allow the serum to run over the surrounding unbroken skin.

Afterwards apply a little simple ointment or oil on a soft rag, which you should have already prepared. The dressing will probably require to be changed twice or thrice during the first day, and less frequently as the surface heals. You may be directed to apply some such preparation as savin ointment to delay the healing of the blistered surface.

DRY HEAT is sometimes employed, as in lumbago, colic, etc. Flannel alone soon loses heat; but if salt or sand be heated over the fire or in an oven, and placed in a flannel bag, it will retain the heat for a long time. This form is most suitable in lumbago, where its own weight is no objection, as the patient can lie on the heated salt or sand. Bran or chamomile flowers are lighter, but do not retain the heat so long. They should be heated over the fire and applied in a linen or flannel bag. In some cases a thin clay tile, which is not very heavy, may be heated, wrapped in flannel, and applied.

COLD LOTION is often applied to the brow in head affections or in certain feverish states. It is a common error to dip a handkerchief or such like in cold water, and having folded it several times apply that to the brow. It speedily becomes warm from contact with the skin, and would require to be continually changed to be of any service. A much better plan is to take one fold of linen, the thinner the better, soak it in water or in vinegar, or in spirits and water, and apply it to the brow. As the water evaporates a greater degree of cold is produced. You must see that the linen is not allowed to become dry.

When we wish a still greater degree of cold we employ ice. As an external application it is used chiefly in head affections. Let us suppose you had to apply it in a case of apoplexy. You would require first an ice-bag. In an emergency (and such cases are always an emergency), and especially in the country, it is well to know that a bladder, such as may be procured at a butcher's, will always be a suitable substitute. Failing that, if you have ordinary gutta-percha tissue and some chloroform, you will be able to make a water-tight bag in the following way.

Having cut a piece of the tissue paper, say

12 inches by 8, fold it once in its longest direction, and then with a camel hair brush, which has been dipped in chloroform, run along the margin between the folds of the open side and of one of the ends. This will cause the opposed surfaces to adhere, and you repeat the process, folding again each edge on itself. In this way a sufficiently strong watertight bag will be made. You next take the ice and break it into small pieces, which is best done by applying a darning needle to the surface and giving it a few taps on the head with a hammer or other weight. Some nurses adopt, I believe, a more wholesale and possibly more expeditious method. They put a piece of ice into a towel and smash it into fragments on the hearthstone. The ice being broken, you put it into the ice bag, filling the latter not more than half full, so as to allow it to lie closely to the head. In the case of the gutta-percha tissue bag you then seal up the remaining side with chloroform as before.

The application will continue ice-cold till the last piece is melted, but not a moment longer.

A Cold Compress may sometimes be ordered. It should be prepared and applied on the same principles as a hot fomentation. But you take cold water as the medium, and in place of flannel a folded soft towel is used. It is just as essential in this case that the macintosh thoroughly overlaps. If it does not, the compress will continue cold, and be worse than useless.

The *Wet Pack* and *Cold Affusion* we shall take up along with *Baths*, the consideration of which must be deferred till next lecture.

QUESTIONS ON LECTURE VIII.

1. Why are bedsores particularly liable to form in a case of paralysis, and on what parts of the body are they most likely to form?

2. What precautions would you take to prevent the formation of a bed-sore?

3. How would you apply a hot fomentation, and why?

4. How would you prepare and apply a linseed meal poultice?

5. Mention what was said regarding a fly blister.

6. You are ordered to apply ice to the head in a case of apoplexy—What steps would you take?

LECTURE IX.

BATHS—THE COLD PACK—COLD AFFUSION—LEECHES—
ENEMATA—HYPODERMIC INFECTIONS—THE ADMINISTRATION OF INTERNAL REMEDIES.

BATHS.—When we speak of baths we generally refer to water as the medium, but a bath may be of any kind. The term in its widest signification includes, indeed, any medium except that by which we are ordinarily surrounded. We have for example vapour baths, compressed air baths, and even earth baths; but we shall only consider here the different kinds of water-baths.

There can be little doubt that a body so universal as water is, must be serviceable for many a useful purpose. It forms, as we all know, an essential part of our food, and almost all animals select it as the chief cleansing

THE TEMPERATURE OF A BATH.

medium. Man would select it for this purpose instinctively, and so we find, as we would expect, that the practice of bathing goes back to the earliest days of the world's history. Whether the practice has grown with its years is another matter.

The question of baths in health, however interesting, is not now before us, and we have simply to consider them as employed for remedial purposes. With this object baths are usually hot or warm. They are generally employed to promote the action of the skin, induce perspiration, relieve pain, or remove the congestion of some other part of the body. In the case of a child suffering from one of the eruptive fevers, a hot bath is sometimes employed to bring out the rash more perfectly. Sometimes by its stimulating action on the skin and sometimes undoubtedly by its cleansing action, it soothes the child and perhaps brings to it refreshing sleep.

In preparing a bath the first thing you have to consider is the degree of temperature you want. Is it to be a hot, a warm, or a tepid bath? Here are the temperatures which these terms respectively may be held to represent:—

Tepid bath,	- -	85° to 90° Fah.
Warm bath,	-	90° to 98° ,,
Hot bath,	- -	98° to 112° ,,

The temperature of a hot bath, you will observe, is from that of the normal temperature of the body upwards to one of most exceptionally high fever, and that of a warm bath, from the normal temperature of the body downwards a few degrees. You need not burden your memory with what is understood to be the temperature of a temperate and a cool bath: in special cases you will have a bath thermometer on which all these terms mentioned have a definite temperature assigned to them. A complete bath is usually of a lower temperature than a partial bath.

To prepare a bath put in the hot water first, and add the cold till the thermometer indicates the required temperature.

The patient, in most cases, will be able to take his bath himself. He should not have far to go, and should avoid all risk of a chill by having a blanket, or similar covering carefully round him, and slippers on his feet. You should be within call.

The length of time the patient should remain in the bath depends on his strength and the temperature of the water. A hot bath is always agreeable and even exhilarating for a few minutes, but if continued unduly, it becomes powerfully depressing even in the case of the strongest persons. Ten minutes is an ordinary time for an adult to remain in a hot bath, and fifteen in a warm bath. Immediately the bath is over, the body should be quickly dried with a soft towel, or a warm sheet may be placed round the patient, and the body dried through it. Let the patient then get to bed at once.

A hot bath is an effectual remedy for flatulent pains in an infant. The child should be immersed in the water to the neck, and should not be in the bath longer than three or four minutes.

A foot bath or *a hip bath* should always be a hot one, and may be continued for fifteen minutes. A foot bath especially, given most commonly to relieve cold in the head, should have hot water added almost continuously, a greater degree of heat being bearable as the temperature of the feet themselves is raised. A tablespoonful of mustard may be added in such cases with advantage.

A mustard bath is frequently employed in the case of children to bring out a rash, or as a counter-irritant in severe bronchitis. A tablespoonful of mustard should be added to a bath large enough for a child, who should be held in it by the nurse till her own arms tingle and smart. (Sydney Ringer.)

A soda bath may be ordered for a case of rheumatism. You simply require to add one pound of carbonate of soda (washing soda) to the bath, which will probably consist of about thirty gallons of water. *A sulphur bath* is formed by adding a quarter of a pound of sulphate of potash to the same quantity of water.

In the case of an adult who is unable to leave his bed, a blanket bath may be administered to induce sweating. A blanket is first wrung out of hot water, and then put round the patient. Over this three or four dry blankets are placed, and the patient lies enveloped in these for about half an hour. The

THE COLD PACK.

surface of the body should then be rubbed dry with warm towels.

The warm bath is sometimes employed to lower the temperature in high fever. The patient may be kept for a quarter of an hour, or longer, in a bath of 95° Fah. In some cases of fever, when the temperature is very high, its reduction may be brought about by the use of cold baths. They have been tried extensively in Germany, but not to a great extent with us. The patient is lifted into a bath of tepid water, and cold water gradually added. It should always be done in the presence of a medical man.

THE COLD PACK is a commoner method with us of reducing temperature. The patient lying on a mattress, on which has been placed two blankets, should have a pillow for his head, and nothing covering him save one blanket. The sheet, having been wrung out of cold water lengthways, should be slipped under the blanket, and placed over and round the back of the patient, who, for that purpose, should be on his side. This having been done the patient can lie round on his other side so as to allow the other, the near, side of the sheet to be completely wrapped round him. The two blankets on which he is lying can then be brought tightly about him, and the blanket originally over him may be added if it is thought necessary. Half an hour is an ordinary time to keep the patient in the pack.

Cold Affusion may be ordered in some cases, for example, of fever, in which the patient complains of severe and persistent headache. This is usually done now by supporting the patient's head over the side of the bed, and from a height of two, or perhaps three, feet pouring cold water upon it, the water being caught in a basin held underneath. The stream should be directed on the spot where the pain is most severe, or otherwise on the brow; generally the patient will prefer to have the water poured on a particular spot. It may be continued for a few minutes, and repeated frequently.

Leeches.—This is the last strictly external application we have to consider. They are applied in the early stages of many inflammatory affections.

The first thing you have to do is to clean the part thoroughly, for the leech is a thorough believer in the use of cold water. It will not bite if the skin be oily, or if there be any strong odour about the patient such as that of tobacco.

Having cleaned the part, catch the leech by the middle with a soft cloth, and lay it on the desired spot. If it does not bite soon, withdraw it gently from the skin, and this will probably make it fasten. But a leech should be handled as little as possible. If it still refuses to bite, the part should be washed with milk, or with sugar and water, or scarified slightly.

On removing the leech do not adopt the routine practice of putting salt about its head. It makes it disgorge the blood certainly, but it hurts the leech, and perhaps kills it. Rather catch it in the left hand, and by a little pressure with the finger and thumb of the right hand carried towards the head you can make it disgorge the blood. It should then be placed in clean cold water.

To encourage bleeding from the bite, you

may be directed to apply fomentations. Should there be, on the other hand, some difficulty in getting the bleeding stopped, remember the general rule, that all the blood which will be about the part must first be removed. The half-dozen applications that will likely, in a private case, have been tried are also to be removed, and a small firm compress of lint applied *just over the bleeding point*, the pad being kept in position with a turn of a bandage. Should this pressure be inadmissible on account of the state of the part affected, you can, by means of a darning needle, pack the leech bite itself with a very small piece of soft linen rag. It can be left so for three or four hours, and will be always successful in arresting the hæmorrhage. I am, of course, supposing an exceptional case where medical assistance cannot be obtained.

ENEMATA or INJECTIONS.—These consist, as the names indicate, of remedies thrown into the system. The term was long restricted to injections into the bowels, but we now speak every day of hypodermic injections, or injections under the skin.

INJECTIONS.

An intestinal enema is employed usually for one of three purposes: to induce movement of the bowels; to check their undue movement; or to administer nourishment. We shall consider each of these three forms.

1. To induce movement of the bowels. For this purpose the injection should be large. A pint at least; sometimes two or three pints in amount. A pint of water with some soap dissolved in it forms a mild enema. If to this a tablespoonful or more of castor oil be added, or a tablespoonful of common salt, a more stimulating action will be produced. To administer it the patient should lie on the left side with the knees drawn up; and the nozzle of the syringe should be introduced within the bowel upwards and backwards. The patient should be directed to retain it as long as possible, and you may aid this endeavour by firmly pressing on the end of the bowel with two fingers in a towel.

2. To check undue movement of the bowels. This is, practically, to check diarrhœa. For that purpose we usually employ a cold starch injection of about two ounces. Laudanum

may be added by the doctor's directions. The injection should always be small in amount, and very gently and slowly given.

3. A nutrient enema. Here the great error commonly made is to give too much at a time. Three ounces slowly administered is as much as the bowel will bear readily, and if frequently repeated that amount for each injection may be too much. If necessary the bowel should be first washed out with a tepid water injection. A good nutrient enema may be made with 2 oz. of beef-tea and $\frac{1}{2}$ oz. of cream, and in some cases $\frac{1}{2}$ oz. of brandy in addition.

HYPODERMIC INJECTIONS.—These are mainly employed to induce sleep or relieve pain. You should know how to give one. See first that the syringe is in proper working order, that the piston runs smoothly yet tightly along the barrel, and that the needle is clean and not obstructed Having affixed the needle to the syringe you fill the latter with the number of minims ordered, estimating the quantity by the numbers, representing minims or drops, which are either on the barrel of the syringe or on the rod of the piston. You then oil the needle. Any part of the body may be selected for giving the injection, as the general effect is not influenced by the choice of a particular spot. The inner surface of the upper arm, where the skin is loosely attached to the subjacent tissue, is as good as any. Having raised the skin well up with the finger and thumb of the left hand, drive the needle quickly and firmly under the skin in a direction almost parallel with the surface of the arm, and then slowly compress the piston of the syringe. Let the needle remain in position for a minute or so after the injection is completed. Carefully wash out the syringe afterwards; blow any fluid out of the needle, dry it, and pass a piece of silver wire through it to prevent it becoming blocked.

And now, lastly, I have to say a few words to you about:—

THE ADMINISTRATION OF INTERNAL REMEDIES.—You will here understand by that, the administration of medicine, which is the old meaning of the term when the care of the sick began and ended with the giving of some drug. Although that is now a comparatively small part of treatment, it is not and never will be an unimportant one; and there are some important questions connected with it which must be noticed.

You hardly require to be told that all that has been said about accuracy and regularity in administration, applies particularly to medicine. It is much more apt to be forgotten than food, which is natural enough; and almost as sure as it is forgotten the idea suggests itself to the nurse that she will just double the dose the next time. In place of removing you only add to your past error, and I simply say that such a thing, as well as the supposed necessity for it, should never occur. I would ask you also to bear this particularly in mind. A nurse should never administer any medicine on her own responsibility, except in the case of an emergency. You may not do much or any harm by merely giving a simple purgative, but why assume a responsibility that is clearly another's duty?

The time of administration has usually a distinct relation to meals, and the medicine is directed either to be given so many times a day or every two, three, or four hours as the case may be. In hospital you acquire a routine as to the giving of medicine, but in private nursing you should have some simple scheme for your guidance, in cases in which the precise hours are not indicated. For example, suppose a medicine is ordered to be given every four hours night and day, you could arrange the hours thus—2, 6, 10 A.M., and 2, 6, 10 P.M. If four times a day you could say, 8 A.M., and 12 noon and 4 and 8 P.M.; or three times a day—9 A.M., 2 P.M., and bedtime. The patient's meals, as I have said, often determine when medicine is to be given. Stomach tonics are usually given before meals. Blood tonics, as they are called, are usually given during digestion; and so also some medicines which are not easily borne by the stomach except after food, for example arsenic, and, in many cases, iron.

Accuracy not only as regards time of administration, but as to the quantity administered, is most essential. Unfortunately the common system of ordering fluid quantities is both inaccurate and misleading. By a tablespoonful for a dose was originally meant half-an-ounce fluid measure. But the difference of opinion as to when a tablespoon is full may represent fifty or a hundred drops, and after all tablespoons are of very different sizes. The modern table, dessert, and tea spoons hold about twice the quantity that their old-fashioned namesakes do, and it is the latter that are meant by the prescriber. Nor is it more accurate to say so many drops. Drops differ in size according to the consistence of the fluid, the shape of the lip of the bottle, and other conditions. It is therefore much better, much safer, always to employ the standard measures, and the table of these you should know by heart.* It is obviously inaccurate to understand by a teaspoonful, one drachm, if a modern teaspoon can with care be made to hold two drachms; or to suppose that a dessertspoonful is equal to two drachms and a tablespoonful to four drachms or half a fluid ounce, if they can be made to hold double their respective supposed equivalents. This is being felt, and

* See Appendix.

consequently the use of standard measuring glasses is becoming more common; and one of the first things all of you should know is how to measure by the ordinary 2 ounce and 2 drachm measures. The former answers well down to quantities of three or even two drachms, but drachm and minim doses should invariably be measured by the latter. It amounts to this, then: if you are told to give half-an-ounce so many times a day you measure a ½ oz. accordingly; if a tablespoonful you should measure a ½ oz. all the same. If you have no measure, all you can do is to make it a small tablespoonful; in the case of a drachm a small teaspoonful.

Never give any part of a mixture without first looking at the label. I would ask you all to teach yourselves that habit: it may prevent many a serious error.

It will do no harm to acquire the habit of giving all mixtures a slight shake before using them, and when pouring them out to keep the labelled side of the bottle up, which will prevent the directions from being blotted with drops of the mixture.

Never allow a bottle to stand uncorked. Volatile mixtures will quickly lose their strength, and others, by the evaporation of the water in them, will actually in a given quantity become stronger. Some should not be exposed to light, for example chloroform, nitrate of silver solution, etc.

I need not tell you that many medicines are difficult to take from their nauseous taste, and some from the form in which they are administered. Pills, for example, are often swallowed with difficulty. If so, they may be put into a small piece of bread and then taken with a little milk or water. Powders if they are not large may be taken within thin pieces of bread. The common grey powder is better given in milk, water, or gruel, than in jelly. As for castor oil everybody has at least one nice way of taking it, by which it is rendered quite tasteless, if you will only try it. We may take their word for it, for I too have an absolutely tasteless way to recommend. Adopt say the common method of putting half-a-teaspoonful of brandy into a tablespoon and filling it up with castor oil; then—let it go well over the back of the tongue, avoiding the front half altogether, and no taste will be felt.

One word as to the administration of a narcotic. If such a drug does not procure sleep as it is intended to do, it will often only excite. Now the tendency to sleep may be thwarted in place of being encouraged by injudicious management. If you are directed to give a soothing draught say at bedtime, then any talking that may be necessary should be got over just before that time, and if other things admit of it the patient should be placed in a new and comfortable position. The draught should then be given, the gas lowered, and the room kept perfectly still. In some such way you will be most likely to procure for the patient refreshing sleep.

QUESTIONS ON LECTURE IX.

1. What is understood to be the respective temperatures of a hot and a warm bath, and with what objects are they usually employed?

2. Describe the method of administering a cold pack.

3. How would you promote and how arrest the bleeding from a leech bite?

4. With what objects are intestinal enemata employed? and mention any characteristic distinction in the administration of each.

5. How would you give a hypodermic injection, say, as a narcotic?

6. What was said regarding the measurement of doses of fluid medicines?

LECTURE X.

CONCLUDING REMARKS—NATURAL QUALIFICATIONS OF A NURSE—THE CULTIVATION OF CERTAIN HABITS—HABITS TO BE AVOIDED—THE RELATION BETWEEN DOCTOR, NURSE, AND PATIENT.

As the medical section of the lectures has been taken last this session, it rests with me now to address to you a few words appropriate to the conclusion of the course. You have had the principles on which you are to act set before you by us; you are now to put them into practice for yourselves. And looking back on all that has been said, the first thought likely to occur to you, one that would certainly occur to an independent and more experienced onlooker, is this, Is it really necessary for us to know all that has been brought under our notice during the present course? It is a question often and very reasonably put by medical men—Should a single symptom of any ailment be explained to a nurse, or should she be taught the treatment, or at least the reason of the treatment of any disease?

Now, even if it could be rigidly determined what is in itself essential for you to know, and what is not absolutely essential, there can be no doubt that the former would lose something of its completeness, something of its force, if the latter were taken away. But we can draw no well-ruled line between the two; they are too completely interwoven. A good nurse will do her work all the more thoroughly that she does it intelligently, and a wise nurse will avoid the only danger that is to be feared, the danger of a little knowledge —of knowledge a little beyond what is absolutely required for her usual and more ordinary duties. To this danger I shall by and bye refer.

But to you as nurses asking yourselves the question, Is it really necessary to know and remember all that we have heard? and to all who think that you are taught overmuch, a sufficient answer to my mind is this, that you can never tell when you may require to act on your own responsibility, you can never foresee the possible emergencies that may at any time confront you. Several of our best known nurses have had their knowledge and skill put to the test amid the countless exigencies of actual warfare, and if, as we all hope, this may never be your experience, there are in a city like ours the no less real and the far more constant forms of disaster that meet us on every side, whether in the struggle for existence or in the conflict with disease and death.

Assuming, then, that these lectures bring to a close your period of probation, and that you are now about to engage in the work of nursing as a profession, I cannot do better than refer to those natural gifts which are most essential to you in your future career. These qualifications deserve and admit of a more definite arrangement than is generally given them; at least there is one that should always be placed first as the most essential and the foundation of all, that is, a love for the work, a devotion to it for its own sake. That must underlie, as it will embody, all the others. Exceptions do occur when the work is undertaken primarily as the means of gaining a livelihood, and the love for it steadily grows, but these do not affect what I believe to be the rule. Certain it is that if your love for the work comes tardily, so will your success, and this will never come if that is altogether wanting.

I would like to put plainly before you what you are to understand by devotion to your work, or rather what you are not to understand by that expression, that you may guard against what I believe to be a mistaken view of it. I avoid what may be termed the sacred aspects of the duty, I leave these untouched when I say, don't be devoted to nursing in the abstract; don't be devoted to the *idea* of it you have formed, or that others may have formed for you, but work for your patients, work for them as individuals, be devoted to the wellbeing of each. In so doing you will not limit the most exalted view of your calling that one can possibly take.

It is only when understood in this sense that devotion to your work implies what is in itself another qualification of a nurse— a kind and loving heart. Many occupations can be carried on independently of such a gift, but not that of a nurse. That will shorten the weary hours of watching, lighten duties in themselves unpleasant, and make you bear with patience the fickle temper, or, it may be, the ungrateful heart. Expressing itself on your countenance, it will be reflected on and caught up by those about you. It will quicken your ear to the cry of want or pain, it will lighten your footstep and soften your touch.

This word, touch, brings us to the next essential qualification I would mention, namely, tact, one by no means peculiarly essential, but still most essential to you in the work before you. Tact is a quality not easily defined; but if we go back to its original meaning we can construct a definition upon it. It means literally touch—the touch of skill and experience. But it has a wider significance; it includes the mental touch, something more complete than the other; not a touch merely, but a grasp—the grasp of the situation. The comprehension of a difficulty, the grasping of it on all sides so that it disappears in your hands. This is tact, and by it alone will you be able to meet the ever recurring and ever varying emergencies that beset your work.

Patience, another important qualification, is indeed a virtue in a nurse. It will doubtless be the result of that devotion to your work to which I have referred; but often it will be sorely tried, even if you possess it as a special gift. In convalescence particularly, when the patient feels his weakness and is more alive to the dull monotony of day succeeding day, is this most likely to be the case. When your ingenuity well nigh fails you in providing some new entertainment for him, then comes the test of your patience.

There are many other natural gifts of great value to a nurse. They are not peculiar to her office however, and are in general demand. Discretion, the recognition of the right course amongst several others. Decision in meeting a difficulty, and firmness in overcoming it.

Gifts such as these, combined with gentleness and a good temper, form an ideal which you must ever keep before you, and to which you must ever strive to attain.

From these natural gifts, which, though natural, undoubtedly admit of further cultivation, we pass on to what may more accurately be termed habits. They are more under the power of the will, and if you possess them to a slight extent they may be strengthened or matured by determined effort.

First of all I would mention order. That is simply having a place for everything, and everything in its place. There is no habit of more extended advantage to you than this. It is a great part of neatness, and like it, looks well; but what is of far greater importance, it enables you to act well. It may prevent many a serious error, or, it may be, dangerous delay. It will help you in any form of emergency, not merely with "an emergency case" as we say, but in a case of general emergency. Suppose, for example, that some evening the supply of gas to the hospital was suddenly cut off, order of a conspicuous kind would enable you to find everything in the dark. Without it you may find yourself in the dark even at noon-day. Its cultivation generally will be the most wholesome discipline to yourself, and pave the way to other habits to which it directly tends.

Punctuality is such another habit. It is just order with reference to time. I referred to its importance in speaking of the administration of food, and do so again in illustration of the general principle. When we speak of a particular habit, we refer usually to an intellectual or moral quality, but we can apply the term also to what is purely physical. The habit of early rising, for example, will depend on the conviction of the advantage or necessity of the practice, but the individual will also find that he will awaken and rise most readily at that particular time each morning; a physical as well as a mental habit has been formed. And so we incline to fall asleep at a particular hour. This applies equally to the taking of food, or rather to what prompts to it, the sensation of hunger. We have then in health a natural physical punctuality; but in disease it is quite different. The appetite is capricious, and feeble at the best. Surely we should throw no obstacle in the way to its return to the natural state. Further, you may find if you neglect this, and delay the giving of a meal, that when it is ready, the patient's appetite is gone; and that means strength gone and time lost. Then, if the body is weak the mind is weakened too. The patient will be far more exacting on your attention, he will fret over your delay, and magnify a few minutes into many.

Profit then by the cultivation of this habit enforced on you here. Essential to the well-being of the whole hospital, regard it as an invaluable training to yourself. It will enable you to contend against the very opposite condition of things that you will meet with in private nursing. For there this special order and regularity are not required as a rule, but only as the exception in the hour of sickness. In some families these habits are conspicuous by their absence in any degree. Such a condition of things you can only meet quietly, yet firmly and effectually, by meeting it naturally; and it is here, in this hospital, as I have said, you must endeavour, by cultivation, to make these habits a second nature of yourself.

Cleanliness and neatness are two of the recognised, I might say statutory, qualifications of a nurse. Their importance is too apparent to require any remarks from me. But as regards your wards, and all that pertains to them, let me just say this, remember you must be as particular—especially in the matter of cleanliness—about those things that usually escape the observer's eye as those that conspicuously meet it. Whether it is desirable that ward cupboards and presses should have glass doors or not, it is absolutely essential that everything that is in them should be kept as if they had. Honesty, truthfulness, and sobriety, I only mention to complete the recognised list. They need only be mentioned.

All these natural gifts or habits to which I have referred you may practise here in hospital without modification or restriction. You possibly hope by and bye to be engaged in private nursing, when you will be brought into contact with those accustomed to be waited on, and who have more regard than your patients here to the manner in which it is done. Now, even that training you can get here, for there is not one manner for the rich and one for the poor. If there is the same law for rich and poor, still more is there the same duty for you to perform in the same spirit towards both. Cultivate, then, from the outset that deportment which will command affection and respect, and you will fit yourself for your work in any household.

There are still some cautions I must give you; some habits to be avoided. Guard against anything like favouritism; you must be impartial in the discharge of your duty. The thankless patient must be cared for as well as the most grateful. Your duty will be a greater pleasure in the one case, no doubt; but even if not pleasant, it is equally your duty.

Never speak about a patient's case in his hearing, or should that be unavoidable, do not do so in a whisper; and never let a patient overhear or learn in any way from yourself what the doctor has not yet thought it right to tell him.

But there is one habit particularly I would have you train yourselves from the very first to avoid, and that is gossiping about your patient's ailments to those whom we may call "outsiders." I have nothing to do with whether you are gossips in the ordinary sense of the term; I speak only of what it is my province to speak of. Make it a special duty to separate what concerns your patients from everything else. Large though your budget of news may be, so large that, without being generous, you feel constrained to share its weight with others, keep distinct what concerns your patient; put it away in a separate part of your head, and keep it there till the doctor comes.

I have discussed sufficiently your general qualifications, and have considered them chiefly in relation to those under your care. I would like now to say a few words to you about your relation to the doctor.

This question, you will understand, is of the very first importance, when you consider what kind of union there is between you and us. It is to do battle with a common and relentless foe, an enemy that in one or other form will prove some day victorious. No duty can command more unity of action, and, from its character, should create a spirit less dependent on, less tolerant of rule and form. At once a battle and a ministry of the tenderest kind, you imperil its very existence by any form of artificial combination, especially if it be one amongst yourselves distinct from us. I do not speak of rules and laws framed for administrative purposes in hospitals. However clamant the question be just now, it is one which does not concern you and me for the present. I speak only of the relation between doctor and nurse as individuals.

Recognising, then, the importance and the nobility of the duties which you share with us, you will unhesitatingly accord to the doctor that obedience and respect which are his due. The latter ought to be reciprocal; the former, I need hardly say, never, and must always be implicit on your part. And it is here that the danger of a little knowledge is recognised. The lessons you have learned and the knowledge you have gained have increased your power of action, and you may be tempted to exercise the influence it has given you. Trained under one doctor, some one of you may forget herself so far as to criticise adversely the practice of another, and, it may be, act on that opinion. If so, you will never make a greater mistake; one more detrimental to yourself and to the vocation you have elected to follow.

But if there is one thing of which I shall venture to speak positively it is this, that this is not a mistake to which the trained nurse is liable. It is notoriously the nurse of no training, who has picked up a scrap of information here and there, often by stealth, as it were, lest she should expose her ignorance; it is she who, because of her ignorance, and in a vain attempt to conceal it, is tempted to arrogate to herself opinions and functions which she is utterly unqualified to form and fulfil. I say this in defence of the present system of training nurses, so far as I am acquainted with it.

But I would earnestly warn you against anything like a vain display of your qualifications. There are still many among the general public who think that the trained nurse must be more difficult to deal with. It must be admitted that the very fact of your being trained, raises in many minds a feeling of apprehension. However they may express the feeling they entertain, it will resolve itself into this — you are trained, specially trained, so much the more are you unlike ourselves, and you are to be one of ourselves for a time. This is no extreme view. I am not speaking of cases where it is assumed that because you are trained therefore you are self-conceited, that you will "put on airs," as it is often termed. Yet, if we recognise the fact of such an extreme opinion as this being sometimes held, we are led to the remedy for all degrees of it. And what is that? You are not going to give up your special training. No. Neither must you give up your old self. You must preserve your individuality, you must shun all mannerisms, you must more than ever be *natural*. Those of you who learn best will least need this advice, but you all require to remember the very general opinion to which I have referred (general, I mean, in the less extreme and not unnatural form which I stated first), and to keep before you the proper, the only remedy.

I must revert, before concluding, to another point bearing upon the relation between doctor, nurse, and patient. I spoke to you at the beginning of the course about the importance of cultivating the habit of observation, to what a wonderful extent it could be cultivated, and how wide, how unbounded indeed, its field. Just because you cannot be expected to estimate correctly the comparative value of the different symptoms, you should endeavour to take note of all. Let none escape you, or if that be too much to expect, let as few as possible be overlooked, and don't allow yourself to be the judge of what is of little moment, and what is of importance.

And not only must you observe, and observe accurately, but you must be accurate in carrying out your instructions, or note exactly to what extent or in what respect

ACCURACY IN REPORTING.

you are unable to do so. If you observe accurately, and act accurately, you will report accurately—there can be no doubt of that; but if you fail in the first two, never hesitate, never be afraid to report accurately wherein you have failed. It is the last point I have to mention; it is of the very first importance. If you fail in that you fail in all.

But you will not fail. Only do your duty to yourselves, and you will do your duty to all, and to the hospital which is, for a time, to be your home. May you so live and so learn within its walls as to maintain its reputation, and make it an ever-increasing means of good.

APPENDIX.

INVALID COOKERY.

RECIPES.

1. TOAST WATER.

THE great point to be attended to in preparing this is not to allow the toast to be overdone. Cut a slice of stale bread, and with a toasting fork hold it a few inches from the fire, turning it frequently till all the moisture is driven off. Then hold it near the fire until it is of a well marked brown colour, but not more, on both sides. Put it now into a jug, and pour over it about two pints of boiling water; cover the jug and allow the water to become cold. Then strain into a clean jug and use within the next few hours.

2. BARLEY WATER.

Having first washed two ounces of pearl barley, put it into a saucepan with two quarts of water. Boil for two hours or more until the barley is quite soft, stirring and skimming occasionally. Strain through muslin and sweeten to taste. If allowable, a little lemon juice may be added, which makes it to most patients a more agreeable drink.

3. RICE MILK.

Wash two tablespoonfuls of good rice, and put it into a saucepan with a quart of milk. Let it simmer gently till the rice is tender, and stir it from time to time to prevent it burning. Sweeten to taste. If allowable, it may be served with black currant jam or stewed apples. Sago, tapioca, etc., are prepared in the same way. If an egg is to be added, beat the white and the yoke separately, and add them to the rice after it has been taken from the fire.

4. ARROWROOT MILK.

Take a dessertspoonful of arrowroot and two tablespoonfuls of water, and mix them well. Add by degrees half a pint of boiling milk, stirring all the time. Then put it into a pan and boil for three or four minutes.

5. SIMPLE BREAD PANADA.

Grate down some stale bread and add sufficient water to form a rather thick pulp. Cover it up and allow it to soak for an hour. Then beat it up with two tablespoonfuls of milk and a little sugar, and boil the whole for ten minutes, stirring all the time.

6. SPONGE CAKE.

Five eggs: the weight of four in sugar, and of nearly three in flour. The flour and sugar must be dry and sifted.

Separate the whites from the yolks. Beat the latter in a large bowl for ten minutes, then strew in the sugar gradually and beat them well together. Whisk the whites to a solid froth, add the yolks and sugar, and when they are well blended stir the flour in gently. A little grated lemon peel is an improvement. Pour the cake into a well buttered mould, and bake for an hour in a moderately quick oven.

7. BEEF TEA.

Cut a pound of lean beef into small pieces; put it into a covered jar with a pint of cold water and a little salt. Allow it to simmer for a couple of hours, but do not let it reach the boiling point till just three or four minutes before taking it from the fire.

8. BEEF TEA IN HASTE.

In an emergency beef tea can be prepared in a few minutes in the following way. Cut the beef into small pieces, which can be done very quickly, and put it in a saucepan not too large. Add a little water, just enough to cover the meat (if it is a small saucepan three or four tablespoonfuls will be sufficient), and a pinch of salt. Place the pan sufficiently near the fire to get a moderate degree of heat, and begin at once to squeeze out the juices of the meat with a strong spoon. Eight or ten minutes of this will be sufficient. Then remove the meat, and allow the beef tea to reach the boiling point for a second or two to take off the raw taste. The beef can be used again for preparing beef tea in the ordinary way.

9. BEEF TEA WITH OATMEAL.

This forms a very nutritious diet. Take two tablespoonfuls of oatmeal, and two of cold water, and mix them thoroughly. Then add a pint of good beef tea which has just been brought to the boiling point. Boil together for five minutes, stirring it well all the time, and strain through a hair sieve.

10. BEEF TEA AND EGG.

Beat the white of an egg to a light froth, and add to it very gradually a teacupful of beef tea or chicken tea, which must be hot but not boiling.

11. SAVOURY CUSTARD.

Add the yolks of two eggs to a cupful of beef tea, with pepper and salt to taste. Butter a cup or jam-pot; pour the mixture into it, and let it stand in a pan of boiling water till the custard is set.

12. MEAT JELLY.

$\frac{1}{2}$ lb. of lean veal. A small veal bone. $\frac{1}{2}$ lb. of lean beef. Half a small chicken. $\frac{1}{2}$ oz. of isinglass. A small wineglassful of sherry. Salt.

Cut the veal, the beef, and the lean of the chicken into small pieces; add half a pint of water, and salt to taste. Put the whole into a clean saucepan and place near the fire for two hours. Put the bones of the chicken and the veal bone into a separate saucepan with one pint of water and a little salt, and let them boil gently for four hours. Now strain the liquor from both saucepans into one vessel, and add the isinglass which has been previously dissolved in a little water. Then strain repeatedly through coarse muslin until the liquor is quite clear. Add the sherry, and pour into a mould, and let the whole be left in some cool place till it is thoroughly set. Then turn it out, and serve cold.

13. CHICKEN TEA.

Take a small chicken, free it from the skin, and from all the fat between the muscles; and having divided it lengthways into two, remove the whole of the lungs, the liver, and everything adhering to the back and side-bones.

Then cut it, bones and muscles, by means of a strong sharp knife, into as thin slices as possible, and having put them into a pan with a sufficient quantity of salt, pour over them a quart of boiling water. Now cover the pan, and simmer with a slow fire for two hours. Lastly, put the pan upon the hob for half an hour, and strain off the tea through a sieve.

14. POACHED EGG CURRIED.

Mix two teaspoonfuls of corn flour with half a teaspoonful of curry powder, and make into a smooth paste with a little cold milk. Boil a teacupful of milk, into which pour the curry paste. Poach an egg in the middle of this sauce, and serve, after cooking, on a slice of toast with the sauce poured over it.

15. WHITE WINE WHEY.

To half a pint of boiling milk add one or two wineglassfuls of sherry; strain through a fine sieve, sweeten with sifted sugar, and serve.

16. JUNKET.

Sweeten with white sugar one pint of good milk. If wine is allowed, a dessertspoonful of sherry is an improvement. Heat to new milk warmth, pour into a shallow dish, and stir in two teaspoonfuls of essence of rennet. This will form a slight curd. Grate a little nutmeg over it, or add a pinch of powdered cinnamon. Serve when white cold. In cold weather the milk should be placed in a warm room to set.

17. EGG AND BRANDY MIXTURE.

Beat up three eggs to a froth in four ounces of cold water, and then add four ounces of brandy. Mix well, and sweeten to taste. A little nutmeg may be added. Give a tablespoonful or so at a time as directed.

18. KOUMISS.

This, which is a form of fermented milk, is much used just now as a beverage, although a somewhat expensive one. A friend informs me that it can be prepared in the following way. To one pint of new milk add three ounces of water, three ounces of old koumiss (for a ferment), and one ounce of a saturated solution of sugar of milk. Put all in a large jug, cover carefully, and set the jug in a warm place for twenty-four hours. By that time a thick crust will have formed on the surface of the mixture; beat this up thoroughly, and mix all well. Then put the whole into champagne bottles, which should be no more than two-thirds full, and cork and wire. Shake the bottles daily. The koumiss will be fit for use in two days; but it is much improved by keeping for about six weeks. It should be drawn off with a tap.

PEPTONISED FOODS.

The researches of Dr. Roberts of Manchester have given a great impetus to the employment of artificially digested food, or *peptonised* food, as Dr. Roberts suggests it should be called. He recommends Benger's preparations of the natural digestive ferments, a little of which requires to be added to the milk or gruel as the case may be, according to the following methods.

1. PEPTONISED MILK.

Dilute a pint of milk with a quarter of a pint of water and divide the mixture into two equal portions. Heat one portion to the boiling point, and then mix it with the cold portion. (This is the simplest way of getting what is wanted, a temperature of 140° Fah.). Now add to this three fluid drachms of pancreatic solution—Liquor Pancreaticus (Benger)—and about twenty grains of bicarbonate of soda; mix well together and set aside in a covered jug and in a warm situation under a "cosey" for an hour or an hour and a half. Then boil for two or three minutes and serve like ordinary milk.

2. PEPTONISED GRUEL.

It may be prepared from oatmeal, wheaten flour, pearl barley, etc., and should be thick and strong and very well boiled. Allow the gruel to cool to a temperature of 140° Fah. (just so hot that it can be sipped without burning the mouth), and then to every pint of gruel add two teaspoonfuls of the pancreatic solution and mix well together. Pour the whole into a jug with a cover, and set it aside in a warm situation for about a couple of hours. Finally, boil it for three minutes and strain.

3. PEPTONISED BEEF TEA.

Mix half a pound of finely minced lean beef with a pint of water and twenty grains of bicarbonate of soda, and let the whole simmer for an hour and a half. When it has cooled down to a temperature of about 140° Fah. add a tablespoonful of the pancreatic solution, and place the mixture in a warm situation for a couple of hours, stirring it from time to time. Then strain off without pressure and boil the liquid for five minutes.

POISONS AND ANTIDOTES.

An emetic is the most universal antidote. To cause vomiting give a breakfast-cupful of tepid water, with a dessertspoonful or more of common salt or mustard, and repeat the tepid water freely. Or you may give one or two tablespoonfuls of ipecacuanha wine in water to an adult: to a child one, two, or, if necessary, three or more teaspoonfuls.

POISONS.	ANTIDOTES.
ACIDS. *Sulphuric (Vitriol), Nitric, Hydrochloric, Acetic.*	Carbonate of soda, chalk or whiting, in water. Gruel or olive oil. All these in large quantities.

212 MEDICAL NURSING.

Aconite,	Emetics. Stimulants, as brandy or strong coffee.
Arsenic,	Emetics. Milk; raw eggs. Any oil; or oil and lime water.
Carbolic Acid,	Raw eggs. Olive oil or gruel in large quantities.
Caustic, Ammonia, Potash, or Soda.	Vinegar and water; lime-juice; olive oil; emetics.
Corrosive Sublimate (or other preparation of Mercury.)	White of eggs; flour in milk or water. Emetics.
Laudanum (or other preparation of Opium.)	Mustard emetic. Strong coffee; cold affusion; continual forced walking.
Lead, *Sugar of*,	Emetics. Epsom salts (one ounce in water).
Morphia and Opium (see *Laudanum*).	
Nitrate of Silver,	Common salt in large quantities of water.
Phosphorus (*in Phosphorous Paste or Rat Poison.*)	Large quantity of water to cause vomiting. A tablespoonful of magnesia in every other draught of water; or give lime water. Do not give oils.
Prussic Acid (*Hydrocyanic Acid.*)	Fresh air; cold affusion; smelling salts to nostrils. Brandy.

TARTAR EMETIC (or other preparation of Antimony.)	Encourage vomiting by copious draughts of tepid water. Then give two or three breakfastcupfuls of tea and milk.
STRYCHNIA, ...	Emetics. Give brandy or strong tea, and get chloroform ready for medical attendant.

WEIGHTS.

gr. j	signifies one grain	
℈.j	,, one scruple	= 20 grains
ʒss	,, half-a-drachm	= 30 grains
ʒj	,, one drachm	= 60 grains
℥ss	,, half-an-ounce	= 4 drachms
℥j	,, one ounce	= 8 drachms
lbj	,, one pound	= 16 ounces

FLUID MEASURES.

♏j	signifies one minim (about one drop)	
fl.ʒj	,, one fluid drachm = 60 minims = one teaspoonful (old size)	
fl.ʒij	,, two fluid drachms = one small dessert-spoonful	
fl.℥ss	,, half-a-fluid ounce = one small tablespoonful	
fl.℥j	,, one fluid ounce = two small tablespoonfuls.	
Oj	,, one pint = twenty fluid ounces	

NOTE.—The numbers are written *after* the symbols, and in Roman characters; thus ʒiv signifies 4 drachms.

GLOSSARY OF MEDICAL TERMS

NOT EXPLAINED IN THE LECTURES.

Abnormal—Irregular ; unnatural.
Acupuncture—The insertion of needles into the tissues as a remedy.
Acute—A term applied to a disease which runs a sharp and rapid course ; opposed to **chronic**.
Albumen—A natural constituent of the tissues of the body; a constituent of the urine in certain forms of disease ; the white of an egg.
Albuminuria—The presence of albumen in the urine.
Alimentary Canal—The whole tube along which the food and its remains pass.
Anæmia—A condition of body depending on a poverty or deficiency of blood.
Anæsthesia—Loss of sensation.
Anæsthetic—That which produces insensibility.
Anodyne—That which lessens pain.
Antidote—That which counteracts a poison.
Antiphlogistic—That which reduces inflammation.
Antispasmodic—That which relieves spasm.
Anus—The termination of the bowel.
Aphasia—Loss of speech.

Aphonia—Loss of voice.
Aqua—Water.
Asphyxia—Interrupted respiration; suffocation.
Atrophy—Wasting.
Auscultation—Listening; usually applied to listening to sounds in the chest.
Autopsy—The opening and examination of the body after death; a *post mortem* examination.
Bronchitis—Inflammation of the air tubes, or *bronchi* of the lungs.
Cardiac—Belonging to the heart.
Catamenia—The monthly discharge.
Catheter—A tube for drawing off the urine.
Chorea—St. Vitus's dance.
Clinical—Belonging to the bed; bedside.
Coma—Deep sleep; insensibility.
Congestion—A state of fulness of blood in the vessels of a part.
Constipation—A confined state of the bowels.
Contagion—Infection by contact.
Convalescence—The period of recovery from an illness.
Costal—Belonging to the ribs.
Diaphoretic—That which causes perspiration.
Diuretic—That which increases the flow of urine.
Effusion—The pouring out of fluid into a cavity of the body.
Emetic—That which causes vomiting.
Enteric—Belonging to the intestines.
Epigastrium—The upper central part of the abdomen; the pit of the stomach.
Epistaxis—Bleeding from the nose.
Expiration—The act of breathing out.
Fæces—The discharges from the bowels.
Fauces—The throat at the back of the mouth.
Febricula—A slight or short fever.

GLOSSARY OF MEDICAL TERMS. 217

Gastric—Belonging to the stomach.
Glottis—The opening into the windpipe.
Hæmaturia—Blood in the urine.
Hectic Fever—A fever accompanying great exhaustion.
Hepatic—Belonging to the liver.
Hernia—A rupture.
Hydrothorax—Water in the cavity of the chest.
Hypogastrium—The lowest part of the abdomen.
Idiosyncracy—A peculiarity of constitution.
Incontinence—Inability to retain; generally applied to the loss of control over the urinary bladder.
Inflammation—A state indicated by redness, swelling, heat, and pain.
Inhalation—The breathing of steam or of some medicated vapour.
Inspiration—The act of breathing in.
Intercostal—Between the ribs; for example, muscles, nerves, etc.
Intermittent—With an interval. Applied to a fever that goes and returns, or to a pulse which misses a beat.
Larynx—The organ of the voice, situated at the upper end of the windpipe.
Laryngitis—Inflammation of the larynx.
Laryngoscope—An instrument by which the larynx may be brought into view.
Laxative—A mild purgative.
Lesion—An injury, or a change of structure from disease.
Lumbago—Pain in the loins or "small of the back."
Lumbar—The loins; the back at the waist.
Malignant—Intractable; incurable.
Meatus—A passage.
Meningitis—Inflammation of the membranes of the brain, or of the spinal cord.
Micturition—The act of making water.

Mucus—The clear, somewhat viscid fluid, secreted by mucous membranes.
Narcotic—A medicine which produces sleep.
Neuralgia—Pain in a nerve.
Normal—Natural; healthy.
Œsophagus—The food-passage which leads to the stomach.
Ophthalmic—Belonging to the eye.
Ophthalmoscope—An instrument with which the interior of the eye can be viewed.
Opiate—A medicine which produces sleep.
Otorrhœa—A discharge from the ear.
Palliative—A medicine which relieves but does not cure.
Palpation—Examination by touch.
Paracentesis—Perforation. The operation of tapping.
Parietes—Walls: for example, the abdominal parietes.
Paroxysm—A fit. A sudden increase of symptoms.
Pathognomonic—Characteristic; applied to a symptom which identifies a disease.
Pathology—The study of the nature of disease.
Pericardium—The bag which encloses the heart.
Pericarditis—Inflammation of the pericardium.
Peritoneum—The membrane which lines the inner surface of the abdominal cavity, and also surrounds the contents of that cavity.
Peritonitis—Inflammation of the peritoneum.
Phthisis—Consumption.
Pleura—The membrane which lines the cavity of the chest and encloses the lung.
Pleurisy—Inflammation of the pleura.
Pleurodynia—Pain in the side.
Pneumonia—Inflammation of the lungs.
Prognosis—The forecast of the course of a disease.
Prolapsus—A falling down of some internal part of the body.

GLOSSARY OF MEDICAL TERMS. 219

Pulmonary—Belonging to the lungs.
Purulent—Consisting of pus.
Pus—Suppurating matter.
Quinsy—Inflammation of the tonsils.
Rectum—The last portion or division of the bowel.
Remittent—Applied to a fever which recedes but does not quite disappear, and which increases again.
Renal—Belonging to the kidney.
Retina—The expansion of the nerve of sight within the eye, on which the images of external objects are thrown.
Rigor—A shivering.
Sacrum—The lowest part of the spine; it is situated between the haunch bones.
Salines—Medicinal salts, for the most part laxative.
Salivation—An undue secretion of saliva.
Sal Volatile—Aromatic spirit of ammonia.
Scybala—Pieces of hardened fæces.
Sinapism—A mustard poultice.
Specific—A medicine which acts specially; hence a certain or infallible remedy.
Sphincter—The muscle which closes and controls the outlet of certain internal organs.
Sphygmograph—An instrument by which tracings of the pulse are taken.
Stertor—Snoring; hence stertorous breathing.
Stethoscope—The instrument used by the physician for examining the chest by auscultation.
Stricture—A contracted point of some tube, or other part of the body.
Subcutaneous—Under the skin; hypodermic.
Suppository—A medicinal preparation made up with fatty matter; usually put into the rectum, where it quickly melts.

Sympathy—A peculiar connection between certain parts of the body, through which these act in harmony.
Syncope—Fainting.
Tenesmus—A straining to empty the bowel when there is little or nothing to be discharged.
Thorax—The chest.
Trachea—The windpipe.
Transfusion of Blood—The injection of blood from the veins of one into those of another.
Ulcer—Any sore or breach of surface; usually accompanied by purulent discharges.
Umbilicus—The navel.
Umbilical Region—The central part of the abdomen, round the umbilicus. Above it is the epigastric region, and below it the hypogastric.
Unilateral—On one side only.
Vertebræ—The twenty-four bones which constitute the spinal column.
Vertigo—Giddiness.
Viscera—The internal organs; more particularly the intestines.

INDEX.

Accuracy, habit of, 194.
Administration of food, 71.
—— in coma, 74.
—— in fever, etc., 73.
—— general principles as to, 75.
Administration of internal remedies, 171.
Air, composition of, 45.
—— impure, in a room, 49.
Albumen in urine, 103.
Aneurism, nursing of, 91.
Antidotes to poisons, 211.
Apoplexy and epilepsy, 113.
—— first aid in, 115.
Arrowroot milk, 200.

Baking as a method of cooking, 70.
Barley water, 200.
Baths, 160.
Bedroom, disinfection of, 135.
—— ventilation of, 50.
Bedsores, prevention of, 141.
—— treatment of, 145.
—— why liable in paralysis, 118.
Beef-tea in diarrhœa, 81.
—— in weakened digestion, 67.
—— to make, 202.
—— to make in haste, 202.
—— and egg, 203.
—— peptonised, 210.
—— with oatmeal, 203.
Blanket bath, 164.
Blister, fly, 153.
Boiling as a mode of cooking, 69.
Brain and mind, 108.
Bread Panada, 201.
—— poultice, 150.
Bright's disease, 97.
Broiling as a mode of cooking, 70.

Carbonic acid in air, 46.
Castor oil, how to take, 176.
Changes in patient to be observed, 15.
Chest, physical examination of, 44.
Chicken-tea, to make, 204.
—— in weakened digestion, 67.
Cleanliness, habit of, 188.
—— in administering food, 72.
Codliver oil, when to give, 64.
Cold affusion, 166.
—— compress, 158.
—— lotion, 155.
—— pack, 165.
Coma, administration of food in, 74.
Concluding remarks, 179.
Conflict with disease, 9.
Cooking of food, the, 68.
Cough, 39.
—— varieties of, 40.
Custard, savoury, to make, 203.

Deaconess Institution, Fliedner's, 4.
Desquamation in scarlet fever, 129, 132.
Devotion to the work of nursing, 182.
Diabetic urine, test for, 105.
Diabetes, 92.
—— diet in, 93-95.
Diarrhœa, diet in, 80.
Diet in debility, 65-68.
Digestion, 59.
—— in the mouth, 60.
—— of fatty principles, 61.
—— of vegetable food, 62.

INDEX.

Diphtheria, 137.
Disease, its nature, 8.
—— nurse's position towards, 10.
Drops, size of, 174.
Dropsy, varieties of, 97.
Dry heat, application of, 155.
Duty of nurse to doctor, 11.
—— to patient, 12.

Egg and brandy mixture, 206.
—— curried, poached, 205.
Enemata, 168.
Enteric fever (typhoid), 122.
—— how caused, 123.
—— symptoms of, 124.
—— treatment of, 125.
—— prevention of, 128.
Expectoration, 41.
—— varieties of, 42.
External remedies, 146.

Facts to be noted, 19.
Fainting, 115.
Fat, digestion of, 61.
Favouritism to be avoided, 189.
Feeding cup, 72.
Fehling's solution, 96, 105.
Fever, administration of food in, 73.
—— enteric (typhoid), 122.
—— scarlet, 129.
—— typhus, 120.
Fish, in weakened digestion, 67.
Fliedner, Pastor, 4.
Flowers in sickroom, 47.
Fly blister, 153.
Fomentations, 147.
Food or diet, 54.
—— administration of, 71.
—— general principles as to administration of, 75.
—— amount taken to be noted, 76.
—— classification of, 55.
—— digestion of, 59.
—— may be given too often, 64.
—— in weakened digestion, 65, 66.
—— milk as, 57.
—— quantity at a time, 66.
—— unsuitable in weakened digestion, 68.
Foot bath, 163.
Fry, Mrs., 3.
Frying as a mode of cooking, 70.

Gastric juice, 60.
General principles as to giving food, 75.
Gossiping, 190.
Gruel, peptonised, 209.

Habits of observation, 13.
—— to be avoided, 189.
—— to be cultivated, 185.
Hæmatemesis, 43.
Hæmoptysis, 43.
Healing power of nature, the, 10.
Hemiplegia, meaning of term, 117.
Hip bath, 163.
Hooping cough, 136.
Hot bath, 162.
Houdin the conjurer and observation, 13.
Howard, John, 3.
Hypodermic injections, 170.

Ice in fever, etc., 74, 126.
—— to head, 156.
Ice bag, to make, 156.
Infection in diphtheria, 137.
—— enteric fever, 123.
—— hooping cough, 136.
—— measles, 135.
—— scarlet fever, 129.
—— typhus fever, 120.
Injections, hypodermic, 170.
—— intestinal, 169.

Jelly, chicken, as diet, 67.
—— meat, to make, 203.
Junket, to make, 206.

Kidney, diseases of, 96.
Koumiss, to make, 206.

Leeches, to apply, 166.
Linseed meal poultice, 150.
Lotion, cold, 155.

Mannerisms to be avoided, 193.
Mastication, 60.
—— importance of, 62.
Measles, 135.
Measure glass, importance of having, 174.
Meat jelly, to make, 203.
Medicine, administration of, 171.
Milk as food, 57, 66.

INDEX.

Milk, to prepare peptonised, 208.
Mouth, how to cleanse, 73.
Mustard bath, 164.
—— paper, 153.
—— poultice, 151.
—— and linseed meal poultice, 152.

Narcotics, to administer, 177.
Nature, healing power of, 10.
Nerves, sensory and motor, 111.
Nervous system, physiology of, 107-112.
Nightingale Fund, 7.
Nightingale, Miss, 6.
Nitrogen in air, 45.
Nurse, natural qualifications of a, 181.
—— to doctor, relation of, 19, 190.
Nurses, opinion regarding trained, 193.
—— supposed over-teaching of, 179.
Nutrient enema, 170.

Observation to be cultivated, 13.
—— special points coming under, 17.
Order, 185.
Oxygen in air, 45.

Paralysis, varieties of, 117.
Paraplegia, meaning of term, 117.
Patience, 184.
Patient, nurse's duty towards, 12.
—— special points to be noted regarding, 17.
Peptonised foods, 208.
Physical examination of chest, 43, 44.
Pills, how to take, 176.
Poisons and antidotes, 211.
Poultices, 149.
Poultice, mustard, 151.
Powders, how to take, 176.
Prevention of bedsores, 141-143.
Pulse, the, 30.
—— to count the, 32.
—— qualities of, 22.
—— and stimulants, 33.
Punctuality, 186.
—— in serving meals, 76.

Qualifications of a nurse, 181.

Raw meat in diarrhœa, 80.
Reflex action, 112.
Remedies, external, 146.
—— internal, administration of, 171.
Reporting, accuracy in, 195.
Respiration, 34.
—— how to take the, 36.
—— character of the, 37.
Rheumatism, 89.
—— heart disease in, 90.
Rice milk, to make, 200.
Rickets, 83.
—— treatment of, 87.
Roasting as a mode of cooking, 70.

Saliva, its effects on food, 60.
Salt, application of hot, 155.
Sand, ,, 155.
Scarlet fever, 129.
—— precautions during convalescence from, 131.
—— prevention of, 133.
—— disinfection of bedroom after, 135.
Scrofula, 88.
Scurvy, 82.
Sickroom, fire in, 50.
—— ventilation of, 50-52.
Sleep and administration of food, 74.
Soda bath, 164.
Soda water and milk, 66.
Sordes, how to remove, 73.
Southey, the poet, 4.
Sponge cake, to make, 201.
Starch poultice, to make, 151.
Stewing as a mode of cooking, 70.
Stimulants, administration of, 33. 34.
Stomach, muscular movements of, 61, 63.
—— treatment of irritability of, 66.
Stools, character of, 106.
St. Thomas's Hospital, 7.
Sulphur bath, 164.
Sympathetic system of nerves, 110.

Tact, 183.
Teaspoons, etc., not reliable measures, 174.
Teeth, how to cleanse, 73.

INDEX.

Temperature of the body, 21.
—— how to take the, 26.
—— when to take the, 25.
Thermometer, description of, 22.
Toast water, 199.
Turpentine fomentation, 149.
Typhoid fever, see Enteric fever.
Typhus fever, 120.
—— prevention of, 127.

Ulcer of stomach, diet in, 63.
Urine, the examination of, 100-105.
Urinometer, the, 104.

Vegetable food, digestion of, 62.
—— in weakened digestion, 67.

Vegetable food, cooking of, 71.
Ventilation, 44.
—— Dr. Parkes' definition of, 47.
—— general principles regarding, 48.
—— of sickroom, 50.
—— of ward, 53.

Wardroper, Mrs., 7.
Warm bath, 162.
What to observe in patients, 17.
Wilberforce, William, 3.
Whey as food, 66.
—— white wine, 205.
White fish as food, 67.
Whispering objectionable, 189.

ROBERT MACLEHOSE, PRINTER, GLASGOW.

www.ingramcontent.com/pod-product-compliance
Lightning Source LLC
Chambersburg PA
CBHW022010220426
43663CB00007B/1030